FIGURES ON FABRIC

Embroidery design sources
and their application

MARGARET SWAIN

Adam & Charles Black · London

First published 1980
by A. & C. Black (Publishers) Ltd.
35 Bedford Row, London WC1R 4JH
© 1980 Margaret Swain

British Library Cataloguing in Publication Data

Swain, Margaret Helen
    Figures on fabric.
    1. Embroidery – History
    I. Title
    746.4′4   TT770

    ISBN 0-7136-2048-X

Filmset and printed in Great Britain by
BAS Printers Limited, Over Wallop, Hampshire

LIST OF CONTENTS

LIST OF PLATES

ACKNOWLEDGEMENTS

It is now more than sixty years ago that the late G. E. C. Tattersall, of the Victoria and Albert Museum, noticed that some of the figures on a Flemish engraving had been used as models for a needlework panel depicting *Lucretia's Banquet* (see Plates 29 and 30). Since then other scholars have added to our knowledge of the printed sources of needlework design, but progress has been painfully slow, and the search, although absorbing, has been tantalising. It has become clear that pattern drawers of the past had a wide choice of prints that they used with happy impartiality, combining figures from one engraving with flowers from another. The search is further complicated by the readiness with which printers borrowed woodcuts or engravings from other publishers or other countries, so that it is rarely possible to assert with conviction whether the original or a later copy was used as model.

This book, the first to be devoted to the subject, is a summary of our present knowledge, and will perhaps encourage others to build on these foundations. A bibliography is not possible, but full references are given at the end of each chapter.

In my own search, I have been given encouragement and help by more friends than I can possibly list, but especially by John L. Nevinson, most generous of scholars, and Donald King, Keeper of the Department of Textiles, the Victoria and Albert Museum. The late Nancy Graves Cabot of Boston, whose pioneering researches went largely unrecognised during her lifetime, not only shared her wide knowledge with me, but offered me an affectionate friendship. I owe a debt of gratitude to Keith Andrews of the National Gallery of Scotland and Elizabeth McGrath of the Warburg Institute for their expert help. Helen Bennett of the National Museum of Scottish Antiquities, and Naomi Tarrant of the Royal Scottish Museum have given me their unfailing enthusiasm and encouragement.

I am deeply grateful to all those who have provided me with illustrations, and to my many friends in the Edinburgh Branch of the Embroiderers' Guild for their suggestions and help in testing the methods of transferring designs to fabric, especially Ann Anderson, Margaret Cross, Sophie Muirhead and Evelyn Wylie; also to Mildred Davis of the American Institute of Textile Arts, and Messrs J. and P. Coats, Glasgow. To my husband, whose active support enabled me to finish this book, I offer my loving thanks.

INTRODUCTION

Embroidery, says the Oxford English Dictionary with its customary directness and clarity, is the art of ornamenting cloth or other fabrics with figures of needlework. But before the needlewoman can start to select her colours, thread her needle and begin the delightful exercise of stitchery, with its varied and intricate rhythms, the figure, or design, must first be chosen. The idea that the design must be created by the needlewoman herself is comparatively modern. Our forbears were untroubled by such a necessity, and copied designs from many printed sources, as this book sets out to show.

The design, once chosen, must be transferred to the material, of the right size. Only then can the needlewoman begin to stitch. She could, of course, buy a pack: material or canvas ready traced with threads supplied. But if this is not the right size or colour, or if she would like something more personal, then she must do it herself, or else commission someone to do it for her. Books on stitchery abound, but very few offer detailed guidance in this vital preliminary process of transferring figures to fabric.

This is no new problem. Throughout the ages, embroiderers, male and female, domestic and professional, have faced the same difficulties: first, the choice of design, then the transferring of the design to material. This book takes an historical view of the ways in which embroiderers of the past have met these problems. They are still valid, but modern methods with some technical improvements are included for the use of the needlewoman of today. It is an attempt to present authentic evidence of the origins and fashioning of these embroidered textiles.

I

FIGURES ON FABRIC

Needlework, of all the arts, is surely the most evocative. The tools—a needleful of thread, with scissors or shears to cut it off, have scarcely changed over the centuries. The skill in using these tools may vary from straight stitches made with a bone needle holding together two layers of cloth, to the sophistication of a Chinese dragon robe, its meticulous stitchery shimmering with silks and gold. The artless cross stitch letters on the painfully worked sampler of a child may touch the beholder more than the figure of a saint on a medieval vestment, even though the saint is worked in the peerless English embroidery called *Opus Anglicanum*. The childish effort evokes instant sympathy, more especially if it is all that remains of the youth of a little girl who became the mother of an ancestor. The saint on the vestment, St Laurence, perhaps, holding his gridiron, is archaic and meaningless to anyone unfamiliar with the story of his martyrdom. The ancient textile remains equivocal and mysterious; only the expert or the needlewoman can appreciate the skill with which the figure is embroidered.

Fortunately, recent research has uncovered some of the background of this medieval needlework, *Opus Anglicanum*, that was so prized on the continent of Europe. The names of some of the embroiderers, Alexander le Settere and others, and their addresses in the City of London, are now known, and show that workshops were well established around 1300 to produce such vestments for export.[1] Capital would have been needed to supply the costly materials that went into their manufacture, and it may be that fresh light can now be thrown on to their methods, their workers, and their designers.

Indeed, all too little is still known of the professional embroidery workshops in Britain, both before and after the Reformation. A medieval Broderers' Guild is known to have existed in the City of London to regulate and maintain standards of work and apprenticeship. In 1561 it was succeeded by the Broderers' Company which received its charter that same year from Queen Elizabeth. Unfortunately, the records of the Company were destroyed in the Fire of London in 1666, and in a later fire. Although still in existence, it has become a City Livery Company, and its members are no longer practising embroiderers.[2] Only one name remains, that of Edmund Harrison, on whose behalf the Broderers' Company petitioned Charles II in 1660. Harrison was then seventy years of age, in poor circumstances, but described as 'the ablest worker living', who had been Embroiderer to Charles I, and had, during the Commonwealth, hidden 'His Majesty's best cloth of state and a rich carpet' to prevent their sale by Cromwell. A picture, now in the Victoria and Albert Museum (T147. 1930), depicting the *Adoration of the Shepherds* is inscribed on the back *Edmund Harrison imbroderer to King Charles made theis Anno doni 1637*.[3] It is one of six known panels that showed scenes from the *Life of the Virgin*. One, roughly two feet square, in the Royal Scottish Museum (1963–62), presents the scene of the *Visitation* and is also dated 1637 on the back (Plate 1). Another, of the *Betrothal of the*

Plate 1. *The Visitation of the Virgin* to her cousin, Elizabeth (Luke I 40). Coloured silk and silver gilt thread on linen. Split and couching stitches. Inscribed on the back *Edmund Harrison Imbroiderer to King Charles m[ade this] 1637*. One of a set. H. 61 × 59 cm. *The Royal Scottish Museum*.

Virgin, is in the Fitzwilliam Museum, Cambridge. Two others were in Corby Castle, near Carlisle. Worked mostly in laid gold, they are evidence of his skill as an embroiderer and his mastery of technique.

It is not suggested that Harrison designed the panels himself, any more than the weaver of a tapestry—or, indeed, the owner of a tapestry workshop—would have designed his own cartoons. A professional embroidery workshop, in England as on the continent of Europe, would have had a designer to draw out the pattern on to the fabric for the embroiderers, (men and women) to work. These designers were no doubt competent draughtsmen, able to sketch out flowers and flourishes, and to arrange them into well-proportioned patterns for the decoration of the object, whether an altar frontal, herald's tabard, horse-trapping or gentleman's waistcoat. They would not, however, be expected to undertake free figure drawing. When this was required, a sketch or full-sized cartoon by an artist would be used, or the figures on a good engraving copied, not only to ensure that the anatomy and proportions were correct, but also to reproduce the posture.

The skilled drawings of Harrison's pictures need cause no surprise. He worked for the court at the same time as the finest Mortlake tapestries were being produced. The Mortlake workshop was set up by Charles I when Prince of Wales, who imported Flemish workmen and continental designers to draw the cartoons. One such designer, Franz Cleyn, or Clein (1582–1658), a German born in Rostock, had visited Italy and then worked for a time in the court of the Danish king, Christian IV, uncle of Charles I. Cleyn came to England, at Charles's invitation, as designer to the Mortlake workshop. One of his outstanding sets was that depicting the story of *Hero and Leander*. Cleyn painted mural decorations in some of the great houses and drew plates for books, such as the large folios of the work of Virgil published by John Ogilby.

Other artists were attracted to the court of the connoisseur Charles I. Some, like Rubens and Van Dyck, left the country before the defeat and execution of their royal patron. Some, such as Wenceslas Hollar, a Bohemian, (1602–1677) returned at the restoration of Charles II to be reinstated, like Edmund Harrison, into the royal service. Hollar, appointed *H.M. Scenographer and Designer of Prospects* by Charles II, was a versatile illustrator, producing maps, portraits, a series of womens' costumes and other subjects that were offered for sale by the printsellers of London. They could be used, like other engravings, as pattern sources by silversmiths, wood or stone carvers, as well as pattern drawers for needlework to be executed in a workroom or in the home.

Engravings could be, and were, used as models by painters and sculptors as well as by craftsmen in silver, wood or textiles. By this means the sketches of great masters could be cheaply obtained and carried from country to country, and the designs could be translated into other media. A graceful small statue of a bagpiper wearing a shepherd's hat, with ankles crossed, by the Florentine sculptor, Gianbologna (1529–1608) is derived from an engraving by Dürer dated 1514.[4] A series of engravings called *The Creation* published in 1604 by J. Sanredam after drawings by the Utrecht artist Abraham Bloemart (1564–1651) were adapted as oil paintings by Spanish artists, Alonso Cano and Juan Antonio de Frias Escalante. Engravings were widely used by silversmiths in decorating bowls, goblets and plaques, either in relief, or chased. In the Netherlands, where some of the most accomplished engravers worked, Christian and mythological scenes were translated from prints on to small metal plaques, or on to stone and marble carvings, to decorate monumental edifices, such as the rood screen of the church, once in Hertogenbosch and now erected in the Victoria and Albert Museum, London.[5] Needlework pattern drawers were therefore following accepted practice in taking Bible scenes by skilled artists, or flora and fauna from books of natural history, as designs intended for the home, the church or for dress.

In the eighteenth century sets of engravings continued to be produced and were used freely by craftsmen. Vases, pillars, flowers, animals, biblical, classical and hunting scenes all provided acceptable patterns for woodworkers, plasterers, painters, potters and metalworkers. Even Roman ruins offered inspiration. The marquetry on some of the most sumptuous furniture used at the French court derives from such engravings. An ingenious and beautiful mechanical table, whose back section rises at the release of a catch, is decorated with a marquetry scene taken from an engraving entitled *Débris d'un ancien Palais Romain*. A cylinder-top desk has panels showing ruins from an engraving by P. F. Tardieu after a design by Pannini (1691–1756).[6]

Similarly, the most sought-after porcelain made in Europe was decorated with designs taken from engravings, and much scholarship has uncovered the sources of the painted scenes that embellish the fragile early products of the Meissen, Sèvres, Bow and Worcester factories. The charming modelled figures of shepherds and shepherdesses, clowns and harlequins are all known to derive from prints. Indeed, a single engraving of *Water* from the *Four Elements* after the Venetian painter Jacopo Amigoni (1675–1752) appears as two white Chelsea porcelain figures: one of the boy holding a fish, the other of the seated girl with a basket. They appear singly on a Doccia tea bowl and saucer, and re-united, as in the engraving, on the lid of a Battersea enamel box. They are shown in reverse on a panel of French wallpaper of about 1770. Moreover, the engraving must have made the journey to China, for their elegant figures decorate cups and saucers made there for the Dutch market, and are now to be found in Europe and America.[7]

From the sixteenth to the nineteenth century woodcuts and engravings have formed a useful reservoir of inspiration for the designer in many fields. Their importance as the source of needlework design was first recognised as long ago as 1918 when C. E. C. Tattersall identified the figures on a large tent stitch hanging, worked in the late sixteenth century, showing *Lucretia's Banquet*, with those in an engraving by the Flemish engraver, Philip Galle. (See plate 29). Other scholars, notably John L. Nevinson, and Nancy Graves Cabot, have added to our knowledge of the printed sources of embroidery design, but their findings are not easily available to the student, and the following chapters offer a summary of our present knowledge, and, it is to be hoped, a challenge to future workers to extend this field.

The idea that an embroiderer ought to create her own original designs is a comparatively recent concept. It arose partly as the result of the writings of William Morris, who held a highly romantic view of the happiness and freedom of the medieval craftsman: 'the free craftsman doing as he *pleased* with his work'. His teachings were propagated by the Arts and Crafts Society, who preached the necessity of a designer being also a craftsman. They believed in the equal importance of all the decorative arts, including embroidery.

In 1885 Francis H. Newbery (1853–1946), a warm admirer of Morris, was appointed Principal of the Glasgow School of Art, and in 1894 a needlework and embroidery class was started by his wife, Jessie Rowat Newbery (1864–1948) who had herself been a student at the School. Other students included Charles Rennie Mackintosh, his wife, Margaret Macdonald and her sister, Frances, who married Herbert McNair (who later taught at the School of Architecture in Liverpool), and Jessie M. King. About 1901 Mrs Newbery began to be assisted by Ann Macbeth (1875–1948) while the latter was still a student. Together they extended the class to include the training of women teachers in elementary schools. These classes were held on Saturday mornings and were entirely voluntary; the teachers who attended them did so in their free time, in order to pass on to their pupils this fresh approach to the teaching of sewing. Ill-health forced Mrs Newbery to retire in 1908 and Ann Macbeth continued in her writing to preach the necessity for simple stitchery and decoration for dress and furnishing, especially when they were made by children or those unable to draw. In her books, children were encouraged to make simple borders with lines of coloured stitches, to create designs by drawing circles round a penny, or a leaf shape. After she retired to Patterdale in the Lake District, Ann Macbeth continued to lecture with enthusiasm to countrywomen in the newly formed Womens' Institutes, persuading them to dispense with bought transfers, and to evolve their own simple patterns by the same means as those she taught to children.[8]

That the designer should also be a craftsman is not perhaps quite the same thing as saying that all craftsmen must make their own designs. Indeed, Morris himself, and his daughter, May Morris, drew out many designs for others to work, either to order, or later, by selling materials ready stamped with silks to work them. (See plate 51.) Mrs Newbery drew out designs for relatives and friends, choosing the silks for working. Ann Macbeth firmly believed that everyone should have a piece of embroidery on hand, and she designed many pictorial panels on silk and linen for others to work, such as the one of St Margaret of Scotland, worked by her youngest sister, Sheila. (Plate 2.) She also sold many designs to Donald Brothers, Dundee, for their stamped linens, and to the firm of Liberty and Co. in London.

In the art schools new generations of students were being trained after the Glasgow pattern. The students, who were selected for their talent for drawing, were taught to regard embroidery as an art form of its own, using fabric and thread instead of clay, metal or paint. They were, quite rightly, encouraged to experiment, to create

Plate 2. *Margaret of Scotland, Saint and Queen*. Coloured silks on satin. The panel was designed by Ann Macbeth, of the Glasgow School of Art, and worked by her sister, Sheila, in 1914. *Miss H. Gooden.*

new textures and new forms, using old techniques in new ways. The quest for originality had now become paramount.

The dilemma of the amateur needlewoman, as opposed to one trained in an art college, has not yet been resolved. Whether she can draw or not, she is exhorted to make her own designs, even when she might prefer to exercise her skills in the satisfaction of meticulous or intricate stitchery, or the selection of subtle colours. It is no more reasonable to insist that someone skilled in embroidery should work only her own designs than it would be to demand that a great singer should perform only music of his own composing. Certainly many amateurs are capable of working creditable designs of their own devising, given sympathetic encouragement and dedicated teaching; the rest must continue to rely, as their ancestors did, on designs drawn out by others.

References

1. Fitch M. London Makers of Opus Anglicanum *Transactions of the London and Middlesex Archeological Society* Vol. 27 1976 pp. 288–296
2. Holford C. *A Chat about the Broderers' Company* 1910. The Company still possesses two embroidered Masters' Crowns of the seventeenth century:
   Nevinson J. L. Crown and Garlands of the Livery Companies *Guildhall Studies in London History* Vol. I No. 2 April 1974.
3. Wardle P. *A Guide to English Embroidery* Victoria and Albert Museum 1970 Plate 43.
4. Avery C. and Radcliffe A. *Gianbologna, Sculptor to the Medici* exh. cat. 1978 no. 135.
5. Avery C. The Rood-loft from Hertogenbosch. Victoria and Albert *Year Book* 1969 No. 1 pp. 110–136.
6. Bellaigue G. de *The James A. Rothschild Collection at Waddesden Manor* Vol. I 1974 Nos 83 and 65.
7. Cabot N. G. Engravings as pattern sources. *Antiques* Vol. 58 Dec. 1950 pp. 479, 480.
   Mannheim E. M. The Shadow of Amigoni. *Antique Collector* Vol. 31 Dec. 1961 pp. 215–220.
8. Swain M. H. Mrs J. R. Newbery 1864–1948 *Embroidery* Vol. 24 no. 4 Winter 1973 pp. 104–107;
   Swain M. H. Ann Macbeth 1875–1948 *Embroidery* Vol 25 no. 1 Spring 1974;
   Swain M. H. Mrs Newbery's Dress *Costume* No. 12 1978 pp. 64–73.

2
THE ARTIST AND THE
PATTERN DRAWER

Although little is known of the designers of *Opus Anglicanum*, some clues as to their methods may be inferred from the embroideries of Italy that have survived in churches undisturbed by the protestant reformation. Even allowing for the wear (and neglect) of centuries, altar frontals and vestments in that country have been regarded as sacred objects and have generally been preserved with more respect than secular dress or textile furnishing.

The artists of Italy have been the subject of searching and intensive study. It is natural therefore, that the drawing on the most outstanding of the early church embroideries should be scrutinised, compared with, and attributed to some well-known artist of the same place and period. An altar frontal now in the Victoria and Albert Museum (T1 1965) formerly in the cathedral on the island of Veglia (now called Krk in Yugoslavia) shows the *Coronation of the Virgin* worked in gold and silks on a background of red silk, mounted on linen and interlined with white paper. Donald King has argued cogently that this altar frontal, made for the cathedral in a Venetian workshop, was designed by the painter Paolo Veneziano about 1330.[1] He goes further, and suggests that the drawing of the features and other details where the embroidery has worn away is so close to that of the master that it could only have been drawn out in Paolo's studio. He quotes *Il Libro dell' Arte* by Cennino Cennini, who lived and worked in Padua:

> Again, you sometimes have to supply embroiderers with designs of various sorts. And for this, get these masters to put cloth or fine silk on stretchers for you, good and taut. And if it is white cloth, take your regular charcoals and draw whatever you please. Then take your pen and pure ink, and reinforce it, just as you do on panel with a brush. Then sweep off your charcoal. Then take a sponge, well washed and squeezed out in water. Then rub the cloth with it, on the reverse, where it has not been drawn on; and go on working the sponge until the cloth is damp as far as the figure extends. Then take a small, rather blunt, minever brush; dip it in the ink; and after squeezing it out well you begin to shade with it in the darkest places, coming back and softening gradually. You will find there will not be any cloth so coarse but that, by this method, you will get your shadows so soft that it will seem to you miraculous. And if the cloth gets dry before you have finished, go back with the sponge and wet it again . . .[2]

The instructions are for artists, not embroiderers. It is clear that in this case, following these instructions, the design is drawn in *grisaille* directly on to the fabric. No colouring is suggested, only shading. There is no mention of a coloured sketch or cartoon to guide the embroiderer who has to work the design.

In Florence, an altar frontal that is contemporary with the Veglia frontal, and has a similar subject, the *Coronation of the Virgin*, bears the maker's name and nationality: *Jacobus Cambi, Florentinus 1336*.[3] Since some of the details on this frontal appear on other Florentine embroideries, it has been suggested that cartoons from different masters were utilised as models for embroiderers to select, without the necessity of their being drawn out on the cloth by the artist himself, as in the Veglia frontal.[4] This would certainly explain the similarity of many of them to the work of established painters.

There is no question, however, as to the identity of the designer of the surviving panels of scenes from the *Life of St John the Baptist*, now in the Museo dell' Opera del Duomo in Florence.[5] A set of vestments was ordered by the Guild of Merchants for the high altar of the Baptistery, and the pictorial panels for the orphreys were designed by Antonio Pollaiuolo (*c.* 1432–98). He was one of two brothers who ran a successful workshop, working as painters, engravers and goldsmiths. Payment of ninety florins was made in 1469 and again in 1480 for 'the cartoons that are being painted by Antonio di Jacopo del Pollaiuolo'. Eleven embroiderers working under a supervisor had been appointed to undertake the work which was begun in 1466 and completed in 1480. Twenty-seven scenes from the orphreys have been preserved. In this case, the painted cartoons supplied not only designs, that could be traced and then pricked and pounced on to the linen ground; they also indicated the shades and gradations of colour to be followed by the gold and silk stitches.

In the Chapel of the Holy Shroud in Turin Cathedral, there is an altar frontal made between 1618 and 1623. It was made by Ludovici Pellegrini, an embroiderer who occupied a position at the court of Charles Emmanuel I of Savoy similar to that of Edmund Harrison at the court of Charles I in London. The frontal is richly padded with gold embroidery, and has medallions showing scenes from the life of the Virgin. It was designed by the Turin artist G. C. Procaccini (1574–1625) and remarkably, the full-scale coloured cartoon, which was cut into sections for the use of the various embroiderers as they were working, has been joined together again and is now in the National Gallery of Canada, Ottawa.[6] As with the Pollaiouolo cartoon in Florence, a tracing of the design would be pricked and pounced on to the cloth in the embroiderers' workroom, and the cartoon preserved for guidance as to colouring.

There are records of other artists drawing designs for needlework. Rubens is reputed to have designed altar frontals, though it may be that engravings after his sketches were used as patterns, rather than full-scale cartoons. (See chapter 4.) Lady Grisell Baillie paid the Scottish artist John Scougal (*c.* 1645–1730) £6. 4. 0 for two portraits and frames, and another £4 for other pictures, some of which still hang at Mellerstain. She also included in her accounts 'For drawing Grisie's peticoat by Scougald 5/- sterling': a design apparently suitable for quilting or other

Plate 3. Lady's white linen handerchief, with the initials A.G. in
one corner. Designed by the French architect Hector Guimard as
a wedding present for his wife, Adeline Oppenheim, whom he
married in 1909. The design shows the elegant lines of Art
Nouveau, and is professionally embroidered. Guimard, who
designed some of the Métro stations in Paris, left there in 1938
and moved to New York, where he died in 1942.
Philadelphia Museum of Art.

needlework.[7] Many artists must have drawn out patterns for friends and relations.
William Blake drew out some gentle hares that were worked by the wife of a friend.

Perhaps the most romantic design drawn by an artist is on the fine white linen
handkerchief in the Philadelphia Museum of Art, bearing the initials A.G. It is
bordered with the swirling lines and stylised flowers of an Art Nouveau design,
worked with professional precision by a Parisian *lingère*. (Plate 3.) It was designed by
the French architect Hector Guimard, designer of some of the Paris Métro Stations, as
a wedding present for his wife, Adeline Oppenheim, whom he married in 1909. It
appears to have been cherished unused.

It was not until William Morris and his contemporaries restored needlework to an honourable place in their decorative schemes for the home and the church that artists and architects began to consider that the design of embroidery could be undertaken in certain cases without loss of dignity by professional men. Until then, more often an unknown draughtsman, anyone who could draw, would be persuaded to transfer the designs to the cloth; or else a professional pattern drawer, one who worked for the domestic or the professional embroiderer, would be employed.

The *London Tradesman* of 1747, written as a guide to careers and prospects, sums up somewhat cynically the pattern drawers' qualifications and prospects:

Pattern-drawers are employed in drawing Patterns for the Callico-Printers, for Embroiderers, Lace-workers, Quilters, and several little Branches belonging to Women's Apparel. They draw Patterns upon Paper, which they sell to Workmen that want them; especially to Calico-Printers, Embroiderers and Lace-Women: They draw Shapes and Figures upon Men's Waistcoats to be embroidered, upon Women's Petticoats, and other Wearing-Apparel; for all which they have large Prices.

This requires a fruitful Fancy, to invent new whims to please the changeable Foible of the Ladies, for whose use their Work is chiefly intended. It requires no great Taste in Painting, nor the Principles of Drawing; but a wild kind of Imagination, to adorn their Works with a sort of regular Confusion, to attract the Eye but not to please the Judgement: though if he has a Painter's Head, and a natural Turn for designing, his Works must have more of Nature, and cannot fail to please better than the wild Scrawls of a mechanical Drawer.

The Profits of this Branch are large enough, and it employs a good many in this City and Suburbs, as the whole Kingdom is furnished with Commodities of this sort from this Place: for I know none of this Branch settled in any other Part of the Kingdom. As to his Education, he requires neither Languages, nor any Knowledge of the Sciences; and if a Boy is found to have any scrawling Disposition, he may be bound [as apprentice] as soon as he has learned to read and write.

It requires no great Stock to set up a Master; so little that, if it was not for want of Acquaintance to employ them, there would be no such thing as Journeyman in this Trade; However, such as are employed in that Station may earn twenty-Five or Thirty Shillings a Week. They are employed most when the Company are in Town; and have a pretty constant Business all the year.

R. Campbell, the author of *The London Tradesman*, did not appear to hold a high opinion of Pattern Drawing as a career: unlike Engraving, in the preceding chapter, it was not 'reckoned among the genteel Trades'.

It was to combat this acceptance of mediocrity in pattern drawing that, in 1760, the Board of Trustees for Fisheries and Manufactures in Scotland set up a Drawing Academy in Edinburgh. The Board of Trustees, a body composed of public men and judges, administered a fund of £2000 annually. This sum was set aside in 1707 after the Union of the two parliaments of Scotland and England, to foster the fishing and linen industries in Scotland; any surplus was used to encourage new industries or inventions. From the first, the Trustees held annual competitions, offering premiums for new patterns suitable for damask weavers.

In order to improve the standard of design in other manufactures, the Trustees appointed an artist, William Delacourt, 'to instruct youth of both sexes in drawing'. The candidates, mostly apprentices, had to be approved by the Board. There is no record of any female student making an application. In 1777 Alexander Runciman (1736–85) was appointed Master. He had spent some time in Rome, and under him the school became an academy for artists after the Italian model, rather than the school of design envisaged by the Trustees. Runciman's successor, David Allan (1744–96) restored the Trustee's academy to its original purpose. He found the classes swollen with 'housepainters and engravers' (some of whom were to become distinguished Scottish artists). He therefore suggested limiting the students to four in each of these branches, in order to make room for 'damask weavers, carpet makers, paper makers for rooms, calico printers, embroiderers, japanners, carvers, coach painters and seal cutters'. Students, who had to be over the age of 13, had to show 'some proofs of genius for drawing' at the end of six months before being allowed to continue for two or three years. One student was refused because he 'had not yet fixed upon any art or manufacture which he proposed to follow', and another because he proposed 'to follow Drawing as a polite Art'.

In 1796, on the death of David Allan, the post of Master was advertised widely, the advertisement stressing the 'principal objects which the Academy is intended to promote and improve. These are Designs or patterns for Linen and Cotton and Flowered Muslin manufacturers, Carpet manufacturers, Paper stainers, Coach and ornamental painters, Carvers, engravers, and for all the ornamental parts of Architecture'. There were two rival candidates, John Wood and John Graham. Wood was appointed, but Graham, an old student of the Academy, was invited to come from London to set up as a private teacher, accepting twenty pupils nominated by the Trustees. It was also suggested by one of the Trustees, Sir William Forbes, that he should offer 'Daughters of Tradesmen and Manufacturers an opportunity of acquiring a thorough knowledge of Drawing, as being a branch of education essentially necessary to such of them as are engaged in the flowering of Muslin, in tambouring, embroidery, and other works of fancy, and likewise to a pretty numerous class of Females who can earn their livelihood as Governesses or Teachers in private families'.

In 1800 Graham was appointed Master of the Trustees Academy, following the dismissal of Woods after a scandal in which it was proved that the paintings he had submitted as proof of his ability to teach were not entirely his own work. Schools of Design were set up in other parts of the United Kingdom. There is no evidence of girls being admitted as students in Edinburgh or elsewhere. They had to be content to receive private instruction, either at school or from a master.

In 1850, one of the Trustees, Cosmo Innes, asked that his daughter might be allowed to copy from the considerable collection of casts that the Trustees Academy had amassed. He suggested that she might be accommodated in a private room in the handsome building (now the Royal Scottish Academy) in Princes Street that the Trustees had erected. The Master of the Academy pointed out that it would be inconvenient to carry casts from one room to another, and, as similar requests might be forthcoming, the Galleries should be reserved for the exclusive use of ladies on Monday mornings between 10 and 12 noon. The Trustees approved the suggestion, until one of their number, the judge, Lord Meadowbank, pointed out the impropriety of allowing the teachers to attend upon ladies in this way, considering it 'highly objectionable, very inexpedient, and open to great abuse'. The project was quietly dropped.[8]

Pattern drawing continued to be a male occupation. In Glasgow, in 1857, the designers of Sewed Muslin (Ayrshire embroidery) were regarded as well-paid, earning 43/10d per week. They designed patterns for shawls and for printed cottons as well as for needlework. By this time, however, there are records of several businesses specialising in embroidery and run by women, often a mother and daughter, such as Mrs and Miss Bowie in Edinburgh, a firm that survived for a century. (See plate 65.) To compete on these terms, one or other of the family had to be able to draw at least as well as their male counterparts.

References

1. King D. A Venetian embroidered altar frontal. *Victoria and Albert Museum Bulletin* Vol. I no. 4 Oct. 1964 pp. 14–25.
2. Cennino Cennini *Il Libro dell' Arte* ed. by Daniel V. Thompson, New Haven 1933 p. 105.
3. Now in the Museo degli Argenti, Palazzo Pitti, Florence. Schuette M. and Müller-Christensen S. *The Art of Embroidery* 1964 Plates 135–139.
4. Cavallo A. S. A newly discovered trecento orphrey from Florence. *Burlington Magazine* No. 693 Vol. CII Dec. 1960 pp. 510–511.
5. Schuette M. and Müller-Christensen S. *Op. cit.* Plates 325, 326.
6. I am indebted to Mr Hugh Brigstocke of the National Gallery of Scotland for information regarding this cartoon.
7. *The Household Book of Lady Grisell Baillie 1672–1733.* Scottish History Society 1911 p. XXVI.
8. *Minutes of the Board of Trustees for Fisheries and Manufactures in Scotland*, in The Scottish Record Office.
   See: Swain M. H. *The Flowerers* 1955 pp. 27–33.
9. Strang J. The embroidered Muslin Manufacture *British Association Reports* 1857.

3
BIRDS AND BEASTS AND FLOWERS

Woodcuts and engravings from natural history

Embroidery and flowers are inextricably associated. In *A Midsummer Night's Dream*, Shakespeare's Helena reminds Hermia of their school-days friendship when they both:

> Have with our needles created both one flower,
> Both on one sampler, sitting on one cushion.

In Scotland the 'Floo'erin' was instantly understood as white embroidery on cotton, though its prosaic trade name was *Sewed Muslin*. Flowers have decorated fabric from time immemorial, from the Orient to the New World; they have furnished the designs for tapestries, silks and embroidery, their fragile shapes and short-lived blooms still recognisable over the centuries. They have been used by the Christian church not only for their intrinsic beauty, but for their symbolism: the purity of the white Madonna lily (*lilium candidum*), lifting up its straight stem high above the earth; the columbine (*aquilegia*), its white spurs resembling the wings of a dove, representing the third person of the Trinity, the Holy Spirit. The Church borrowed much of its symbolism from classical mythology, giving the symbols a Christian significance in place of their pagan associations. The pomegranate which appears on many ecclesiastical vestments conveys the idea of the universal church by the unity of countless seeds within one fruit. For the Greeks, it was the symbol of Persephone, carried off to the underworld, and in spite of the importunities of her mother, Demeter, the goddess of agriculture, only allowed back to earth for eight months each year, because she had eaten pomegranate seeds during her imprisonment.

The lotus flower, so exquisitely embroidered in silk on a Chinese robe is a Buddhist symbol of purity, borrowed from India. We can only guess whether the stylised flower on a Coptic embroidery had a religious significance, or if the even more stylised cat on a pre-Columbian embroidery of South America was a domestic or sacred animal. Since we no longer perceive their symbolic meaning, they are judged solely on a superficial level as decorative patterns.

Mary Stuart, Queen of Scots, is still a romantic figure even after four hundred years since her execution on February 8 1587. Her skill in needlework is legendary, although only a few surviving panels may now be safely attributed to her. The *emblems* (pictorial devices representing an idea), with their Latin mottoes, require detailed explanation, otherwise their meaning is lost upon the modern spectator. Their significance can only be understood against the events of her stormy life. The flowers she chose to embroider are mostly heraldic: the lily of France, the rose of England and the thistle of Scotland. Many of the panels bearing the Queen's cypher show strongly drawn birds, beasts and fishes, now regarded as merely curious or quaint. Today the choice may seem arbitrary, but some at least can be shown to have had a profound meaning for her. The designs, drawn out on canvas by her embroiderer, and outlined in black silk, are copied closely from books of natural history that were already in her lifetime supplanting the bestiaries and herbals of the middle ages. These books, with their handsome woodcuts, were an attempt to classify the flora and fauna of the known world from observed specimens. They form the beginnings of modern scientific inquiry.

The authors of three of the books used as patterns for Mary's needlework were all physicians. Conrad Gesner, a Swiss, maintained a correspondence with learned men and naturalists in many countries who reported and sent specimens. In 1551, he published in Zurich the first of his four folios on fishes birds and mammals.[1] It was republished several times, and the woodcuts were used to illustrate other books, notably Edward Topsell's *Historie of Four-Footed Beasts* published in London in 1607. Pierre Belon, a French physician, almost the exact contemporary of Gesner, published in 1555 in Paris *La Nature et Diversité des Poissons*, and *L' Histoire de la Nature des Oyseaux*, in which some of Gesner's woodcuts appear, whether lent or pirated is not clear. Another physician, Pietro Andrea Matthioli, who died of the plague in Trento in 1577, wrote a commentary on the *Materia Medica* of Dioscorides, the Greek physician of the first century. Matthioli's *Commentary* was intended for use by other physicians and herbalists, and was illustrated by wood-cut reproductions of his own drawings, and by those of other scholars placed at his disposal. Many editions were published and it was translated from Latin into Italian, French, German and Bohemian. All these books offered well-drawn models for designers, not only of needlework, but for silversmiths and painters as well.[2]

One of the most engaging of the panels bearing the initials of the Queen of Scots is the unmistakable Toucan labelled *A Byrd of America*. (Plate 4.) The black silk of the plumage has perished, so that it is possible to see the inked lines on the canvas, following closely the woodcut of the *Pica Bresillica*. Plate 5 is from Gesner's *Icones Animalium*. This might justly be dismissed as a quaint choice on the part of Mary Stuart, until it is remembered that in 1557, the year before Mary's marriage to the Dauphin, there was a disastrous French expedition to the mouth of the River Plate. A survivor, Jean de Lèry, wrote an account *Voyage fait en la terre du Brésil*, in which he described the toucan and its feathers, made into garments by the natives. Years after she had left Edinburgh, a paper of feathers and 'the beik of a foule of India or Brasile'

Plate 4. *A Byrd of America* Coloured silks on
canvas. Cross stitch. One of the panels on
the green velvet hanging at Oxburgh Hall,
Norfolk, that bears the initials M R (Maria
Regina) for Mary Queen of Scots. The black
silk used for the Toucan's plumage has
perished, revealing the inked lines drawn on
the canvas beneath. The design is taken
from the woodcut illustration in a book of
natural history. See Plate 5. *The Victoria and
Albert Museum on loan to Oxburgh Hall.
Crown copyright reserved.*

were listed among her possessions, perhaps curiosities given her by one of the party.[3]

The books of Belon, published in Paris during her stay there, must also have been familiar to her, especially his treatise on the Dolphin, for one panel shows a leaping dolphin, taken from the woodcut. The needlework shows the fish against the rippling blue of the sea, with an escutcheon bearing the letters M R below a royal crown. It is labelled in English *Delphin*, but if the French name, *le dauphin* had been given, its poignant meaning would have been made clear. In 1558, Mary had married Francis, the Dauphin of France. The fish is a visual pun. (Plates 6 and 7.)

Plate 5. *Pica Bresillica* (Toucan). Woodcut from *Icones Animalium* published by Conrad Gesner in Zurich, 1560 edition. *The University of Edinburgh.*

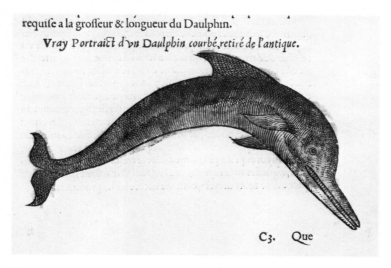

requiſe a la groſſeur & longueur du Daulphin.

Vray Portraiɔt d'vn Daulphin courbé,retiré de l'antique.

C3.   Que

Plate 6. *Un Daulphin* (Dolphin). Woodcut in *L' Histoire naturelle des estranges poissons* by Pierre Belon, Paris 1551. Tinted with sepia watercolour. Mary Stuart's first husband was Francis, Dauphin ('Daulphin') of France whom she married in 1558. *The National Library of Scotland.*

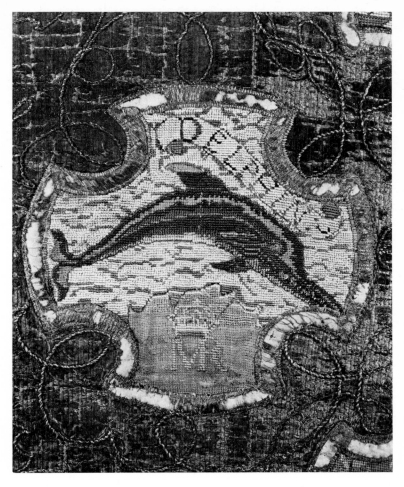

Plate 7. *Delphin* (Dolphin). Coloured silks on canvas. Cross stitch, with the initials M R beneath a royal crown for Mary Queen of Scots. The design is taken from a treatise on the Dolphin by Pierre Belon published in Paris in 1551. *The Victoria and Albert Museum on loan to Oxburgh Hall. Crown copyright reserved.*

Plate 8. Panel showing a turnip. Coloured silks on canvas. Cross stitch
with the intials E.S. for Elizabeth, Countess of Shrewsbury ('Bess
of Hardwick') and the motto *Eventus Rei in Manu Dei* (Success is
in the hand of God). One of the panels applied to the green velvet
'Shrewsbury Hanging' at Oxburgh Hall, Norfolk. *Victoria and Albert
Museum on loan to Oxburgh Hall. Crown copyright reserved.*

Other panels on the green velvet hangings, now at Oxburgh Hall, Norfolk, are
inscribed E S for Elizabeth, Countess of Shrewsbury, wife of Mary's custodian
during her captivity in England. Mary and 'Bess of Hardwick' were on good terms
during the earlier years, and the earl in a letter recorded their sitting together

RAPVM ROTVNDVM.

Decocta Rapi tem ac fluxar Decocto pod tritoque rapo, atque radici rofaceum cera quefcat, exulcer eius decoctæ mandu tidotis, & theriacis, p runt, anodyna uocan nena falutare eft: ue conditum, minus al appetentiam recreat tur. † Frutex eft in mofus, læuis in cacu titudine, aut maiora tis: cùmque eorum i liqua fpectatur, qu bet. in qua femina intus alba. Addit detergendam cuten mur: præfertim qu lolij farina, fieri fol

RApum in Ital apud Infubre nio, ac Iulic tur: deinde menfe O berauerit, è terra e tur genere, feffile, ris mandauerit Plini erraticum effe. N ex tam paruo femine magna radix, ut ea tenas libras pendat

Plate 9. *Rapum Rotundum* (Turnip). Woodcut in *Commentarii*
. . . (Commentaries on the Materia Medica of Dioscorides) by
Pietro Andrea Matthioli published in Venice 1570. *The Royal
College of Physicians, Edinburgh.*

'devising works'. One panel marked E S derives from Matthioli's *Commentary* and shows, not a flower or herb, but the *Rapum rotundum*, the turnip, elegantly embroidered in an octagonal medallion with the Latin motto *Eventus Rei in Manu Dei* (Success is in God's hands). (Plates 8 and 9.) The choice of design and motto[4] may seem quaint, even amusing, but so far no one has subjected the panels signed E S to the same close scrutiny as those bearing the cypher of Mary Queen of Scots. The Greek Dioscorides described the turnip as of use as a poultice for mules, and as food for men in the Alps where corn was scarce, but by the time of Matthioli, the *Naveau blanc de jardin* was already being cultivated in France as a vegetable. It was still a comparative novelty in England, like the green pea, another vegetable popular as a design for Elizabethan needlewomen. It is possible the turnip had as much significance to Bess of Hardwick as the dolphin to Mary Queen of Scots. At Hardwick Hall itself, a similarly shaped panel signed E S shows leeks, taken from the same handsomely illustrated edition of Matthioli's *Commentaries* published in Venice in 1565. This book was not listed among those belonging to Bess at her death in 1608. It may have belonged to the physician in attendance on Mary Queen of Scots.

In the sixteenth and seventeenth centuries, engravings and books of natural history abounded, for the edification of the scholar, to amuse the collector of curiosities and to furnish patterns for craftsmen of all kinds, including embroiderers. This was the golden age of the engraver, with the Netherlands leading in the production of prints on all subjects, from the religious to the profane, from maps of the world to detailed drawings of a flower or an insect. The engraved plates were

Plate 10. The Mellerstain Panel. Coloured silks and wools on canvas. Tent stitch. Worked in 1706 in Edinburgh by Grisell and Rachel Baillie, the two daughters of Lady Grisell Baillie, under the supervision of their governess, May Menzies, whose initials are also on the panel. The birds, beasts and flowers are all copied directly from a book that May Menzies had inherited from her grandmother. The centrepiece shows the figure of *Smelling* from engravings of the Five Senses, bound with the book. 33 × 49·5 cm. *Lord Binning.*

bought, more often pirated, by other publishers, especially in England. One series of engravings, bound into a vellum cover, was bought as a present for his wife Katherine Logan by an outspoken Scottish minister, the Rev. Oliver Colt, of Inveresk. She bequeathed it to her granddaughter, May Menzies, governess of the two daughters of Lady Grisell Baillie in Edinburgh, and they utilised the designs of birds, animals and insects to make a fine tent stitch picture in 1706.[5] (Plates 10 and 11a.)

The volume *A booke of Beast Birds Flowers, Fruits, Flies and Wormes exactly drawn with their Lively Colours truly Described* was published by Thomas Johnson in 1630 in London. It is well produced and well printed, but the designs are all borrowings from other publications. The animals were mostly borrowed from engravings by Adrian Collaert, published in Antwerp. Some of the flowers came from the *Hortus Floridus* of Crispin van de Passe, published in 1614 in Arnhem, while others, such as the rose, were copied from the exquisite engravings of Joris

Plate 11a. Page from *A book of Beast Birds Flowers Fruits Flies and Wormes* published by Thomas Johnson in London, 1630, the engravings borrowed from many sources. Designs were selected from pages of this book for the Mellerstain Panel (Plate 10). The rose above the lion appears over the swan in the needlework. The plums have been inserted upside-down top right. The arrangement of the page shows clearly how a flower is often drawn larger than a beast in these needlework pictures. The motives are all traced from the book on to the canvas. *Lord Binning.*

[9]

A Rose

mould much, wash them throughly in the liquor, then boyle the
liquor againe, and strayne it, let it coole, then put it to your
Barbaries againe.

Conserve of Barbaries.

Take your *Barbaries*, pick them clean in faire branches, and
wash them clean, and dry them on a cloath, then take some other
Barbaries, and boyle them in *Clarret*-wine till they be very soft,
then straine them, and rub them so well through the strainer, that
you may know the substance of them, and boy'e up this matter
thus strained out, till it be very sweet, and somwhat thick, then set-
ting it by till it be cold, and then put in your branches of *Barba-*
ries into gally pots, or glasses, and fill it up with the cold Syrupe,
and so shall you have both Syrupe, and also *Barbaries*, to use at
your pleasure.

B 2   *Of*

Plate 11b. *The Rose* from *A Book of Fruits and Flowers*
published by Thomas Jenner, London, 1656. He may have
been Thomas Johnson's successor. Here the same rose is
used to illustrate *A conserve of Roses.* The rose was copied
from a book of engravings by Joris Hoefnagel published in
Frankfurt in 1592. *The British Library*.

Hoefnagel, published in Frankfurt in 1592. The same rose (Plate 11b) appears as illustration in *A Book of Fruits and Flowers* under the imprint of Thomas Jenner (possibly a successor to Johnson) in 1656. It is a book of receipts for the housewife, with such delights as *A conserve of Roses, How to preserve Barberries, To roste a Shoulder of Mutton with Lemmons,* and *Sweet Bagges to lay amongst Linnen,* as well as *A very good Medicine for the Stone.*

The stock of other printsellers and publishers, active in London over the same period as Johnson and Jenner, and later, show that many of their wares could be used, and were often intended to be used, as embroidery designs.[6] The Overtons, father, son and grandson, flourished from 1629 till after 1707 in the vicinity of St Bartholomew's Hospital. Peter Stent published at the same address from 1643 to 1667 and Robert Walton in St Paul's Churchyard advertised in 1677 a book *The Whole View of Creation in Eight Parts; being a book of Beasts, Birds, Flowers, Fish Fruit, Flyes Insects, containing a hundred and thirty half sheets of paper neatly cut in Copper.*

Prints of use to needlewomen comprised, of course, only a tiny part of their business. Stent's trade card of 1662[7] shows a formidable list of portraits, maps, books on penmanship and architecture, and such useful publications as *Twenty two plates of five Columes, for Masons, Carvers, Artists . . .,* and *Small pieces of the King, Queen, etc. for to adorn Tobacco boxes, much in use.*

It may be that some of these printsellers also sold linen or satin already drawn for embroidery, since the motives on the many small needlework pictures, satin cabinets, and mirror frames, show the same flowers, birds and insects as those on the printed sheets. The draughtsman who re-drew these motives from the engravings of other publishers would find no difficulty in drawing them on fabric instead of paper. Unfinished pieces show the inked lines, drawn in with a sure hand.

These prints of birds, beasts and flowers continued to be utilized as pattern sources well into the eighteenth century. The Mellerstain panel, made under May Menzies' direction, was executed in the reign of Queen Anne from a book published in 1630 containing engravings made as early as 1592. When the lion and the leopard went out of fashion, succeeding generations worked sheep and cattle, dogs and birds in their place, taken from pastoral prints of a slightly later date than the Johnson book, though they were often distinctly old fashioned by the time they came to be used as needlework patterns. This was immaterial. A charming pastoral scene was worked by Faith, the young granddaughter of Governor Jonathan Trumbull of Connecticut. She was born in 1769, and the panel was probably worked about 1785, and intended as a chimney piece. It combines a shepherdess and young lovers with a bird cage, taken from an engraving after Nicholas Lancret, who died in 1743. There are other shepherds, and a milkmaid from an engraving after Nicholas Berchem (1620–83). The same milkmaid had been used as an embroidery design by her aunt, another Faith Trumbull, some twenty-five years before.[8]

Flowers never went out of fashion. New introductions were slow to appear: the passion flower, the auricula and the blue ipomaea only began to be seen after 1750.

By then, the education of young ladies, in Britain and New England alike, included the sketching of flowers, and if the young ladies lacked talent, a governess, brother or friend could generally be found to make a graceful drawing, or a professional pattern drawer could be sought.

Botanical illustrations of the eighteenth century have scarcely been explored as possible sources of contemporary needlework design. The splendid series by Robert Furber *The Twelve Months of Flowers* with their vases of opulent blooms, have been identified by Katherine B. Brett as the source of the design of the painted bedcovers called *palampores* made in India for the English market around 1730 and 1740.[9] It may well be that these same plates, designed by the Flemish artist Pieter Casteels, could have served as patterns for the floral chair covers, with their curving tulips and paeonies covering the canvas, that were popular at the same period.

The Victorians demanded realism in their embroidered flowers. The study of botany and horticulture had become a polite pursuit: it was the era of Curtis's *Botanical Magazine* (1787–1920) and *The Botanical Register* (1815–47), as well as countless other flower books illustrating not only garden flowers, but the wealth of new and exotic plants brought from far-off lands. These publications were the nineteenth century successors to the botanical woodcuts of Matthioli and the engraved flowers in the *Hortus Floridus* of Crispin van de Passe. The Victorian needlewoman did not, however, need to trace the flowers on to canvas. The Berlin designs on squared paper, that began to be sold in London in 1809, offered flower patterns that could be counted out and shaded with a greater degree of realism than ever before. The rose, the lily, the auricula and the passion flower could be instantly recognised, wherever the needlework was mounted: on a *priedieu*, a screen, or a pair of gentleman's slippers.

References

1. *Icones Animalium*. This was identified by Donald King as the design source of many of the Oxburgh panels.
2. Gesner used the well-known woodcut of the rhinoceros by Dürer, with its fictitious dorsal horn. This was reproduced in ceramics, tapestry, plaster work and silver. It is not certain, after 1607, whether the woodcut derives from Dürer, Gesner or Topsell. See: Clarke T. H. 'The Iconography of the Rhinoceros from Dürer to Stubbs' in the *Connoisseur* Sept. 1973 pp. 2–13 and Feb. 1974 pp. 113–122.
3. Thomson T. (ed. by) *Collection of Inventories of the Royal Wardrobe and Jewelhouse* Edinburgh 1815, p. 238.
4. The motto, probably from the *Adagia* of Erasmus, but going back to the Greek of Pindar (born about 522 B.C.) may have been a copy-book maxim. It is uncertain whether Bess of Hardwick knew any Latin.
5. Swain, M. 'The Mellerstain Panel' in *Apollo* July 1966, pp. 62–64.
6. Nevinson J. L. 'Peter Stent and John Overton, Publishers of Embroidery Designs' in *Apollo* XXIV no. 143 Nov. 1936, pp. 279–283. See also, for a scholarly summary of design sources: Nevinson, J. L. 'English Domestic Embroidery Patterns of the Sixteenth and Seventeenth Centuries' in *Walpole Society* Vol. XXVIII 1939–40.

7. Bodleian Library, Oxford. Gough Maps 46.160.
8. Cabot N. G. 'Engravings as Pattern Sources' in *Antiques* Vol. 58 Dec. 1950 pp. 476–481.
9. Irwin J. and Brett K. *The Origins of Chintz* H.M.S.O. pp. 99–100.

4
SEARCH THE SCRIPTURES
Bible illustrations

From the dawn of Christianity, there has been an impulse to enrich churches and vestments with embroidered representations of Christ, His Mother and His saints. This impulse for religious decoration can be found long before the dawn of Christianity. The Book of Exodus tells us that the sacred Tabernacle, carried by the Israelites in the wilderness, was hung around with curtains of blue, of purple and of scarlet, wrought with cherubim. For people dependent on speech rather than the written word, such images had to be immediately perceived. The cherubim, the painted glass Evangelist in a window, the embroidered saint on a vestment, each was known by his dress or symbol: the angel by his wings, St Luke by the winged ox, Mary Magdalene by her long hair and jar of ointment. Originality was not required. The figures of the holy ones had to be instantly recognisable. What was demanded was skill in craftsmanship using the richest materials possible in the service of God.

We, who depend on captions for our photographs, and a spoken commentary for our films, have forgotten how to recognise such symbols, and gaze uncomprehendingly at these early embroideries, without understanding what they portray. The tiny equestrian figure, no more than nine centimetres high, on a Coptic embroidery of the ninth century (Plate 12), a figure with burning eyes and a striking similarity to the late Emperor Haile Selassie of Ethiopia (himself a member of the Coptic Church), no longer suggests St George to us. The picture would have been readily intelligible to any member of the Coptic or eastern church, where St George was popular and venerated. Nearer home, the fiercely galloping knight in armour, in the fragment of *Opus Anglicanum* worked about 1330 (Plate 13) appears to us now as a spirited secular drawing, worked in silks with superlative technique. There is no halo, no dragon. Only when we read in a scholarly note[1] that it is related to the figure of St George on a thirteenth century cope at Uppsala, do we begin to realise it is the same warrior saint. Without the written word, we are blind to its significance.

The artists who drew these designs remain anonymous. Even during the renaissance in Italy, when the artist began to achieve a personal reputation, few

Plate 12. *St George*. Coloured silks on linen.
Straight and split stitches. Coptic embroidery
of about the 9th century A.D., probably part of
a vestment. St George was greatly venerated in
the Coptic church. About 9 cm high. *Cleveland
Museum of Art, Ohio.*

pieces can be attributed with certainty to any individual painter. Even less is known
of the embroiderers who translated the artists' sketches into needlework, though the
evidence of embroidery workshops in the City of London making *Opus Anglicanum*
for export, offers new hope that more information may be uncovered by scholars
about this legendary period.[2]

The introduction of the printing press into Europe in the fourteenth century had
as profound an effect as television in our own day. Ideas and images, conservative or
revolutionary, could be duplicated and disseminated across frontiers and class-
barriers. Bible illustrations were no longer confined to the churches or the
manuscripts of the wealthy. The woodcuts were mostly small and easily portable,
and the sheets could be carried from town to town, from country to country.

Some of the earliest were the *Biblia Paupera*, the poor man's Bible, or perhaps,

Plate 13. A Knight, bearing red crosses on his trappings, probably *St George*.
Silver and silver-gilt and coloured silks. Underside couching and split stitch
(*Opus Anglicanum*). This fragment has been cut from a larger piece. 21 × 21 cm.
About 1320–40. *The Rector, Stonyhurst College, Lancashire.*

more exactly, the poor preacher's Bible, since they appear to have been designed for
the use of friars and other preachers without the resources of a library. They
portrayed, in crude woodcuts, the teaching of the Church on the scriptures. They
were arranged in three columns, with the Old Testament character or incident
showing a fore-runner of Christ, his teaching, or the sacraments. Some are more
instantly obvious than others. Abraham's willingness to sacrifice his son Isaac at
God's command, is shown to the left of the Crucifixion. On the right, Moses holds
aloft the serpent of brass set on a pole, which restored life to those who had been
bitten by serpents: 'Every one that is bitten, when he looketh upon it, shall live'. On
another page, Joseph, cast into the well by his brothers, appears beside the laying of
Christ in the tomb, with Jonah being thrown to the whale on the other side.

But by the year 1500 these *Biblia Paupera* had already been supplanted by Bible picture books that followed the order of the books in the Old and New Testaments. The splendid Cologne Bible, published in that city around 1478 by Heinrich Quentel, had 123 lively woodcuts measuring 19 × 12 cm. The pictures still followed the design of the earlier manuscript illustrations, even to the labelling of the figures, but the sharp outlines of the wood block gave them vitality and impact. Other printing centres were quick to follow, and Bible histories, often with the name of the illustrator on the title page, were produced in the Netherlands, Germany, France and Italy.[3] They supplied a great need, for the study of the scriptures by the laity was an insistent demand by those who wanted the reform of the Catholic church, and by the founders of the Protestant reformation.

In 1553 a small Bible picture book was published in Lyons, a flourishing commercial city on the trade route between the Netherlands, Germany and Italy. The book, *Quadrins de la Bible* was published by Jean de Tournes, who employed a local artist, Bernard Salomon (1508–61) to illustrate the verses by Claude Paradin. Salomon's elegant long-legged figures, set in an airy European landscape, became deservedly popular. An English translation[4] was published that same year, as well as one in Spanish, followed by German, Italian and Flemish versions. The vignettes, one to each page with the verse below, were copied by other publishers, and were used as patterns for needlework for the next hundred years or more.

A set of three bed valances from Balhousie Castle, Perth, the home of the Earls of Gowrie before 1600, is now in the Metropolitan Museum, New York. They show the story of Adam and Eve, from the creation of Eve to the drudgery of life after the expulsion from Paradise, drawn from six woodcuts of *Quadrins de la Bible*.[5] The scenes have had to be adapted from tiny rectangular vignettes measuring 10 × 7 cm to long narrow canvas panels to fit around two sides and the foot of a four-poster bed. The lean elegance of the figures is sacrificed, but they faithfully reflect the attitudes and vitality of Salomon's drawing, occasionally stepping out of their frame, with a head or foot drawn into the enclosing border, giving an unexpected liveliness to the scene.

Another set of these long narrow valances of the same period, possibly French, is in the same museum. They show incidents from the life of Moses taken from Salomon's woodcuts: some faithfully copied, the others freely rendered to fit the altered space.[6]

In Switzerland, two of the characteristic linen embroideries worked in white, brown, and blue linen thread on white, have identifiable scenes from the woodcuts of Bernard Salomon. One, in the Museum Schwab, Bienne, dated 1555, shows the story of Esther and Ahasuerus. Another dated 1569 bearing the arms of the Convent of Muni, Argovia, has four New Testament scenes: the *Presentation in the Temple* follows the Lyon woodcut closely, the other three scenes are more freely adapted.[7] In Zurich is an embroidered carpet, either German or Swiss, dated 1606 with Old Testament scenes taken from the same source, in oval frames.[8]

Other European countries found these small books a source for embroidery

Plate 14. *Tobias and the Angel*. Woodcut by Bernard
Salomon in *The True and lyvely Historyke
purtreatures of the Woll Bible* with verses in English.
Published by Jean de Tournes, Lyons, France 1553.
6 × 7·5 cm. *The National Library of Scotland*.

patterns. A linen cloth embroidered in silks, now in Malmö, Sweden, was made in
the 1570s when that area was still Danish, and shows scenes from Salomon's Bible
pictures. Dr Georg Garde has shown how many of the surviving cloths of that period
made in Denmark owe their designs to other printed Bible and natural history
books.[9]

Salomon's illustration of Tobias drawing the fish from the river at the bidding of
the Angel (Plate 14) has been used for a page of a small book, worked in coloured silks
on vellum in a double-faced technique, so that each side is alike. The book, with its
richly embroidered binding, is Spanish, probably made in a Franciscan convent
about 1662. (Plate 15.) The fish, with gaping jaws, the kneeling Tobias and the

Plate 15. Page from an embroidered book, the margin
strengthened with looped silver wire. Silks on vellum, alike on
both sides. The scene is a mirror image of the woodcut by
Salomon (Plate 14). Tobias seizes the large fish from the Tigris,
the small black and white dog that accompanied him is in the
lower right corner. Above Tobias is an inscription *Aprehende
branchiam piscis et trahe eum* (Seize the fish's gills and draw it
forth), and below the Angel: *Ego sum Raphael Angelus* (I am the
Angel Raphael). Probably worked in a Spanish convent about
1660. 14 × 11·5 cm. *Museum of Fine Arts, Boston (Elizabeth Day
McCormick collection).*

commanding figure of Raphael with his staff and haversack are all reproduced. The dog with curly tail which accompanied them is shown lapping the water at Raphael's feet. It is embroidered in black and white silk and stands beneath the fantastic scrolling stem of the flowers that encircle each page of the book: even that of the Crucifixion. The same illustration of Tobias was used for a tent stitch panel, surprisingly lacking the dog that is included in the scriptural account, for usually these details are faithfully followed. The panel, embroidered probably sixty years earlier than the Spanish book, was in the collection of the late Sir Frederick Richmond.

Another rich quarry for those searching for the origin of scriptural designs in needlework is to be found in *Thesaurus Sacrarum Historiarum Veteris Testamenti* published in 1585 by Gerard de Jode (1521–91) in Antwerp, that fountain of prime engraving. These full-page engravings, roughly 25·5 cm wide by 19 cm high, with a Latin caption, would have been sold either loose or bound. Understandably the bound copies are those that have survived. A volume in the British Museum has in addition been hand-coloured. Many of the engravings are unsigned, but the majority are after drawings by Martin de Vos (1531–1603). Nancy Graves Cabot identified some forty-two embroideries in America and Britain that derive from de Jode's *Thesaurus Sacrarum*.[10] In addition, ten of the twenty-nine Old Testament pictures collected by Sir William Burrell now in Glasgow are taken from the same engraved source.

These small pictures were worked in tent stitch, on canvas, or in silks and metal thread on a white satin that has a green selvedge, the embroidery sometimes padded and raised. They have survived in such numbers that it seems evident that they could have been obtained, drawn for working, in shops — perhaps the same shops that sold the engravings.

The lids and sides of needlework caskets of the seventeenth century also show these Bible scenes. Such a casket in the Metropolitan Museum, from the collection of Judge Untermyer, shows scenes from the story of Esther. Inside is a tray for pens and a sand container for drying ink. Printed at the base of the tray is the notice *Sold by John Overton at the White Horse Inn*. John Overton was a printseller in the City of London, who was in business from 1667 to 1707.[11] *Joseph and his brethren* also taken from de Jode's engraving, decorate the lid of a similar casket in the Whitworth Art Gallery, Manchester. The box contains an engaging note, written by Hannah Smith who made it, reminding herself that she began it in Oxford in 1654 and finished it in 1656, when she was almost twelve years of age. It is unlikely that Hannah thought that her casket with its note would survive for more than three centuries, but her example and her note is to be commended to every needlewoman. The box was made up in London, perhaps in the shop where the ready-drawn satin was bought. These caskets are so similar in design and construction, even to the location of the 'secret' drawers, that they undoubtedly stem from a common source.

Scenes from the Bible would appear eminently suitable for small pictures to hang upon the wall, especially if they were worked by young ladies as part of their education, in an age when the Bible was so familiar and vital a part of it. To use the same illustrations for chair coverings would seem incongruous to modern taste. Two handsome chairs at Temple Newsam, Leeds, made around 1740, have covers of canvas work with flowers and central medallions depicting *Hagar in the wilderness* and *Jacob wrestling with the angel*.[12] A wing chair in the Metropolitan Museum has the unlikely scene of the baptism of the Ethiopian eunuch by Philip from the *Acts of the Apostles*.[13] Another, of the same period, in the Burrell Collection, Glasgow, is enlivened by two unrelated Old Testament incidents on its back: the feeding of the prophet Elijah by the ravens, with above, Susanna and the Elders, a mirror image of de Jode's engraving.

In 1738 Rebecca Hornblower (1722–75) completed a tent stitch cover for a wing chair, signing and dating it, to the pleasure of textile historians, as well as her own descendants. The cover has been remounted on a modern frame. It bears a striking all over design of bold flowers and rich foliage. At the top the prophet Jonah, in a glowing saffron robe, is seated gratefully beneath the gourd tree, waiting for judgement to fall on the wicked city of Nineveh.[14]

Plate 16. Chair with embroidered cover, the back and seat entirely covered in canvas worked with coloured wool and silk. Tent stitch. Back: *Jacob's dream of the heavenly Ladder* (Genesis XXVIII 12) Seat: Isaac greeting Rebecca. Chair about 1750, the covers may have been worked earlier. One of a set of eight chairs. The design follows very closely an engraving of Nicholas Visscher (see Plate 18.) *The Lady Lever Art Gallery, Port Sunlight.*

Impofita faxo Jacob ceruice quiefcens   Aligeros fchalas videt inire choros.   Gene. 28.

Plate 17. *Jacob's Dream.* Engraving by Gerard de Jode after M. de Vos from *Thesaurus Sacrarum Veteris Historiarum Veteris Testamenti*, published in Antwerp 1585. This would appear to be the source of the chair back (Plate 16) drawn in mirror image, but see Plate 18. 19 × 26 cm. *The National Library of Scotland.*

All the chairs in a set of eight in the Lady Lever Art Gallery, Port Sunlight, have seats and backs completely covered with large well-drawn scriptural incidents. One depicts on its back Jacob's dream of the heavenly ladder. (Plate 16.) The scene appears to be taken in mirror image from de Jode's engraving. (Plate 17.) However, the same design appears, with Hebrew letters in place of the Almighty, in mirror image in a volume published about 1660 in Amsterdam by Nicholas Visscher. (Plate 18.) Since this is much nearer to the date of the chair cover, made after 1700, it is more likely that the later engraving was followed. This shows that it is necessary to be cautious in accepting that all these designs stemmed from one or two well-known books. A delightful needlework picture on satin also survives with the same design, but embellished with flowers and insects from other sources, the sleeping figure of Jacob watched by an immodest shepherdess. (Plate 19.)

Visscher's volume also contains two engravings after Sir Peter Paul Rubens, and these have been used by whoever drew out the design of the chair covers on to the

Plate 18. *Jacob's Dream*. Double page engraving by Nicholas Visscher published in Amsterdam about 1660. This is a very close copy of de Jode's engraving, enlarged, in which Hebrew letters have replaced the figure of God in the earlier print. It is from this engraving that the chair back derives. The design of other chair covers in the set are taken from this volume. *British Museum, Dept. of Prints and Drawings.*

canvas. One shows the *Visitation*, from a preliminary sketch for a wing of the great Deposition altarpiece in Antwerp Cathedral. The other shows the *Judgement of Solomon*, a favourite subject for small needlework pictures of the period.

A painting by Rubens of *Herod's Feast*, now in the National Gallery of Scotland (Plate 20) shows Salome receiving the grisly reward for her dancing from a dejected Herod. In a needlework panel now in the Metropolitan Museum New York, the scene is reproduced with great skill on satin, within a medallion surrounded by decorative details elegantly spaced and worked in silks, metal and painted purl. (Plate 21.) These details, the cherubs' heads and the animals at each corner, are to be found on innumerable small English embroideries of the seventeenth century. Although the needlework follows the painting so closely, it shows the difficulty of attempting to pin-point the engraving that served as a model for the draughtsman who sketched the design on to the satin. Obviously the London pattern-drawer could not have seen

Plate 19. Needlework picture *Jacob's Dream*. Coloured silks with some feathers on a satin ground. Third quarter of the 17th century. The figures of the main scene have been drawn from the Visscher engraving (Plate 18) by a pattern drawer, and rendered with some freedom by the domestic needlewoman who embroidered the panel; the shepherdess and the animals are copied from other engravings similar to those in Thomas Johnson's book (Plate 11). Note the relative size of the carnation above Jacob's head. 28 × 42 cm. *Simon Redburn.*

the painting. It was finished in 1633 or 1637 and was already in Naples by 1640. An engraving was made by Schelte A. Bolswerte (1585–1659) from which other paintings were made, but these show additional figures to the left, that do not occur in the needlework, nor in the original painting. The engraving moreover, is in mirror image. An unusually large engraving was made by Francois Ragot (1638–70) with a correct view. Could this be the one used for the embroidered picture?

Although it may be confidently asserted that all the domestic needlework designs showing scriptural subjects worked in the seventeenth and eighteenth centuries must derive from prints, copied by a pattern drawer who may not have been skilled at figure drawing, it is impossible to be dogmatic as to the precise engraving that is followed. This is because the engravers themselves borrowed freely from other publications, sometimes line for line, sometimes in mirror image, often taking the central figures and placing them in a different landscape. The more popular these

Plate 20. Painting *The Feast of Herod*, Sir Peter Paul Rubens. Painted about 1633 or
1637–8, it was in a collection in Naples by 1640. Copies exist showing extra figures at the
left following an engraving by Schelte a Bolswerte. *The National Gallery of Scotland.*

Bible histories became, the greater was the temptation to pirate the pictures.
Printsellers in London were particularly prone to borrow in this way: not only Bible
illustrations, but flowers, animals and mythology can often be traced back to a
continental source. Thus, Visscher's *Biblia Sacra*, published in Amsterdam in 1660,
reproduced many of de Jode's Antwerp engravings of 1585, as well as Rubens'
Judgement of Solomon. This latter reappears in a tiny volume *History of the Old and
New Testaments in verse with one hundred and twenty cuts* published by Samuel Keble
at the Turks Head, Fleet Street, London, in 1694. With so many models to follow,
even a country needlewoman could produce a recognisable image of the Sacrifice of
Isaac, or the Finding of Moses.

Plate 21. Needlework picture *The Feast of Herod*. Coloured silks, silver and gold thread and painted purl on white satin. This picture follows the painting very closely, though the needlewoman has changed the negro's head into that of a maidservant. By keeping so closely to the painting, the pattern drawer appears to have followed not the engraving by Bolswerte with its extra figures, but one by Francois Ragot (1638–70) with a correct view of the painting. English. Third quarter of the 17th century. 42·5 × 53 cm. *Metropolitan Museum of Art, New York. Gift of Irwin Untermyer.*

References

1. King D. *Opus Anglicanum* Exhibition catalogue Victoria and Albert Museum 1963 No. 74.
2. Fitch M. 'London Makers of Opus Anglicanum' in the *Transactions of the London and Middlesex Archeological Society* Vol. 27 1976 pp. 288–296.
3. Strachan J. *Early Bible Illustrations* Cambridge University Press 1957.
4. *The true and lyvely historyke purtreatures of the Woll Bible* by Jean de Tournes MDLIII.
5. Cabot N. G. 'Pattern Sources of Scriptural Subjects in Tudor and Stuart Embroideries' in the *Bulletin of the Needle and Bobbin Club* Vol. 30 1946 nos. 1 and 2 pp. 3–17.
   Standen E. 'Two Scottish embroideries in the Metropolitan Museum' *Connoisseur* Vol. CXXXIX 1957 p. 196.

6. Standen E. 'A Picture for every Story' *The Metropolitan Museum of Art Bulletin* Vol. 15 April 1957 pp. 165–175.

7. Trudel V. 'Swiss Linen Embroidery' *Ciba Review* 79 Basle 1950 pp. 2875–2893.

8. Cabot N. G. *op. cit.* p. 17.

9. Garde G. *Danske Silkebroderede laerredsduge fra 16 og 17 arhundrede* Copenhagen 1961.

10. Cabot N. G. *op. cit.* pp. 56, 57.

11. Nevinson J. L. 'Peter Stent and John Overton, publishers of embroidery designs' *Apollo* XXIV no. 143. Nov. 1936 pp. 279–283.

12. The Jacob design was taken from *Biblia Sacra Veteris et Novi Testamenti* published in Amsterdam by Nicholas Visscher about 1660, the engravings after several artists, some borrowed from de Jode.

13. Acts. VIII 26–39 deriving in part from *Novi Testamenti dn. Jesu Christi* Frankfurt 1627 illustrated by Matthew Merian of Basle.

14. Jonah IV 6. The chair is now at Aston Hall, Birmingham.

5
WHAT MEN OR GODS ARE THESE?
Myth and allegory

For more than eighteen centuries the educated man in Europe was familiar with Latin, the language of the Roman empire, the Catholic church, and European scholarship. Serious writings, theological, philosophical or scientific, intended for international readership, were all written in Latin. Works that profoundly affected the thought of their time, Calvin's *Institutes of the Christian Religion* (1536), Harvey's observations of the circulation of the blood *De Moto Cordis* (1628) and Sir Isaac Newton's exposition of the theory of gravity *Principia* (1687) were intended for perusal by the educated, and therefore published in Latin. Calvin, however, took the precaution of translating his *Institutes* into his native tongue, French, in 1541, in order that those who lacked the benefit of a classical education, such as women and artisans, should be able to understand the new doctrines. During the Reformation the translation of the Bible into the mother tongue had given the common people an opportunity to study and to interpret the Scriptures. These translations had given vitality and flexibility to the native languages of Europe, but this had been paralleled by a revived interest in the pagan literature of Greece and Rome, and every scholar was expected to know the classical authors.

Schoolboys were taught to construe the works of Latin authors, and to compose verse in the classical metres. In the same way as Bible pictures had been published to illustrate the Scriptures, and to attract those who could not read, so publishers issued large and small illustrated volumes of stories from the classical authors. They were in fact often the production of the same publisher. Jean de Tournes in Lyons, whose Bible picture book *Quadrins de la Bible*, illustrated by Bernard Salomon, was to be used so often to provide patterns for needlework, followed it in 1557 by a small easily handled volume with elegant woodcuts by the same artist, surrounded by decorative borders showing incidents in the *Metamorphoses* of Ovid, the Latin writer and poet (43 B.C.–A.D. 18).[1]

The *Metamorphoses*, a poem in fifteen books, is a collection of tales dealing with transformation—of chaos changed into harmony, of humans who became trees or animals or stars. Chaucer and Shakespeare both borrowed from the *Metamorphoses*.

Indeed, so widely were these stories known that everyone could laugh at Bottom and his friends in *A Midsummer Night's Dream* who gave their heavy-handed performance of the familiar story of Pyramus and Thisbe, bringing in all the details of the fate of the star-crossed lovers, even to the chink in the wall through which they whispered.

Bernard Salomon's woodcuts for the *Metamorphose d'Ovide figurée* published in Lyons were not the first: there had been picture books with somewhat stiff illustrations printed in Paris and Venice before 1557, but the freshness and vitality of Salomon's figures, set for the most part in airy landscapes, made them deservedly popular, and their success also invited copying. The book was reprinted several times, and was pirated as well. The figures, slightly altered as drawn out by other engravers, appear in editions published in Germany and the Netherlands.[2] Like Salomon's Bible vignettes, they made delightful patterns for needlewomen. The story of Europa, carried off by Jove when he was disguised as a bull, appears in Salomon's vignette with the maiden seated on the swimming bull, her fluttering

Plate 22. Panel bearing the arms of a Cardinal. Velvet, silks and metal thread ornamented with embroidered scrolls in gilt thread, with applied panels of canvas worked in silks. Tent stitch. The panels show scenes from the *Metamorphoses* of Ovid. These are Top: Orpheus charming the animals with music. Middle row (left to right): 1. Mercury and Herse. 2. Europa 3. Ganymede 4. Pyramus and Thisbe. Bottom row: 1. Apollo and Marsyas 2. Narcissus 3. Perhaps Atalanta 4. Apollo and Daphne. *Musées royaux d'Art et d'Histoire, Brussels. Photo. A. C. L. Brussels.*

Plate 23. Detail of Plate 22. *Mercury and Herse* (top).
Mercury refused admittance to Herse's chamber by
her sister, Agluros. The design derives from the
woodcut by Bernard Salomon, or one of his imitators
(see Plate 24). (Below) *Apollo and Marsyas.*

garments floating in the breeze, while her attendants cry out protestingly on the
shore. A version worked in tent stitch on canvas is at Hardwick Hall, Derbyshire,
with the initials E.S. for Elizabeth Shrewsbury prominently displayed. The design,
coming from a book published at Lyons while Mary Queen of Scots was still living in
France, may, like the turnip (Plate 8) and the other designs copied from Gesner and
Matthioli, have been worked while the Queen of Scots was in the custody of the Earl
of Shrewsbury, and while Mary and Bess of Hardwick sat amicably together
'devising works'.

Plate 24. Woodcut *Mercury and Herse* in *Metamorphose d'Ovide figurée*
first published by Jean de Tournes, Lyons 1557, illustrated by Bernard
Salomon. This, which is probably nearer to the embroidery than the
original woodcut, is from an edition published in Paris in 1585 by H. de
Marnes. 4·3 × 5·5 cm. *The Warburg Institute, London.*

Salomon's *Europa* appears also on a charming satin embroidery, perhaps a bed-
valance, now in the Metropolitan Museum, New York.[3] Another version appears on
a handsome hanging, now in Brussels[4] (Plate 22) consisting of seven small panels of
canvas work, each in a scrolling flowered border, applied to a backing of red velvet,
bearing the arms of a cardinal. Each picture shows an incident from the
Metamorphoses. The majority are taken from the woodcuts of Salomon, or from one
of his imitators. Europa is easily recognised; Orpheus, Ganymede, Narcissus gazing
at his reflection in the water, Daphne, pursued by Apollo, being changed into a bay
tree, are all depicted, together with the tragic end of the love story of Pyramus and
Thisbe. An unusual choice is the story of Mercury and Herse. Mercury fell in love
with Herse, but was refused admittance to her chamber by Herse's sister, Agluros,
who demanded a heavy weight of gold for the privilege. Poisoned by Envy at the
bidding of Minerva, she sat in the doorway blocking the entrance and was turned into
stone. (Plates 23 and 24.)

The story of the nymph Arethusa, who, one hot day, bathed in a stream and was
pursued by the river-god Alpheus, until she was transformed into a fountain, is yet
another tale recounted by Ovid. A needlework picture in the Victoria and Albert
Museum (Plate 25) follows the copper plate engraving by Crispin van de Passe

Insequitur flagrans Arethusam veste carētem | *Sed lassata fuga, fer opem mihi Delia, clamat:*
Alpheus, timidis passibus illa fugit. | *Clamantem spissa Delia nube tegit.*
Crispin van de Passe figurauit et excudit.   *Ouid. Metam. lib. 5.*

(1565–1637) published in 1602.[5] The needlework picture is English, probably made in the second half of the seventeenth century, and is one of a large number whose design can be traced to specific engravings. (Plate 26.)

Fashionable rooms in great houses were hung with woven tapestries showing not only scenes from the Scriptures, but incidents in the lives of gods and goddesses, and nymphs and their lovers. At Hardwick Hall in 1601 there were thirteen pieces of tapestry depicting the story of *Gideon*, which the Countess of Shrewsbury had bought second-hand in 1592; there were three panels of the parable of the *Prodigal Son*, and, in the Withdrawing Room, four panels of the *Story of Abraham*. In addition to these edifying subjects, there hung in the High Great Chamber 'sixe peeces of fayre tapestrie hangings of the Storie of Ulisses Eleven foote deepe', and in the splendid Pearl Bedroom 'fyve pieces of hangings called the planetes': a set showing gods and goddesses presumably called the Planets because of their influence over men. By the end of the seventeenth century, tapestries showing scriptural subjects were going out of fashion. The palace of Holyrood house in Edinburgh was refurbished and rebuilt in the reign of Charles II. The inventory made in 1685 listed four sets of tapestry: the *Story of Diana*, the *History of Cyrus*, the *Destruction of Troy*, and some hangings of 'Forrest work'. No scriptural subjects were displayed.

Furniture covering also followed the trend. Although as we have seen, some needlework chair covers of the eighteenth century still surprisingly (and almost defiantly) depict stories from the Bible, more sophisticated seat furniture displayed classical themes, no doubt following the French fashion. A set of seven chairs made for Stoneleigh Abbey, Warwickshire to celebrate its completion in 1726 have exceedingly well drawn needlework designs from the *Metamorphoses* of Ovid: *Europa*, *Leda and the Swan*, *Pyramus and Thisbe*, and the *Rape of Helen*.[6] An opulent gilded French set, of which a settee and two armchairs are now in the Royal Ontario Museum, Toronto, is upholstered in fine tent stitch of silk and wool. They are dated to the *Regénce* period: the first quarter of the eighteenth century. Medallions on the backs show incidents from the *Metamorphoses*: on the settee, for instance, there are Pyramus and Thisbe, Bisaltis, to whom Neptune appeared in the shape of a ram, and another pair of ill-starred lovers, Procris and Cephalus. The designs derive from an edition of the *Metamorphoses* published in Antwerp in 1606 by Peter de Jode, illustrated by Antonio Tempesta (1555–1630).

Plate 25. Needlework picture *Alpheus and Arethusa*. Coloured silks and metal purl on white satin. In an oval medallion the nymph Arethusa, pursued by Alpheus, is changed into a fountain by the goddess Diana (shown with bow in the clouds). The design follows the engraving by Crispin van de Passe (see Plate 26). English mid 17th century. 26 × 33·5 cm. *Victoria and Albert Museum*.

Plate 26. Engraving *Alpheus and Arethusa* by Crispin van de Passe published in 1602. The naked Alpheus has been clothed in the needlework picture. *Victoria and Albert Museum*.

Plate 27. Chair with gilded frame, from a set
of twelve bearing the stamp of Pierre Bara, a
Parisian *ébeniste*. The covers are worked in
coloured silks on canvas. Tent stitch. The
ground is in two shades of yellow, suggesting
damask. The back shows Jason slaying the
dragon that guarded the Golden Fleece.
About 1770. *The Earl of Mansfield.*

Another handsome set of twelve French chairs was brought from Paris by Lord
Stormont, who was appointed British Ambassador to the court of Louis XVI in
1772. An urbane and knowledgeable man, he was plainly enchanted by French taste,
for he collected furniture and ornaments during the six years he served as
Ambassador in Paris. Many of these have found a home at Scone Palace, Perthshire,
for he became the second Earl of Mansfield on the death of his uncle the great judge.

The chairs are gilded and bear the stamp of Pierre Bara, a cabinetmaker who
started in business in 1758. The covers are remarkably unfaded, worked in coloured
silks on canvas, the ground patterned in two shades to imitate damask. The designs
on the backs of the chairs show a light-hearted variety of scenes, some theatrical,
some with Chinoiserie figures. On one, however, Jason is depicted, with red cloak

Plate 28. Engraving *Jason and the Golden Fleece* from *Metamorphoses en rondeaux* published in Paris 1676 by Le Brun, illustrated by Francois Chauveau and S. le Clerc. This plate is from an edition printed in Amsterdam by Abrah. 7 ×8·5 cm. *The National Library of Scotland*.

and feathered helmet, cutting down the Golden Fleece from the tree guarded by the dragon. (Plates 27 and 28.) The design derives from yet another popular version of the *Metamorphoses*. This was entitled *Metamorphoses en rondeaux*, with a tiny vignette on each page and a verse in French underneath: a book certainly for ladies and not for scholars. It was published in Paris in 1676 and illustrated by Francois Chauveau.[8]

The covers, like the chairs, are French, and it has been suggested that they were worked at St Cyr, the school for girls founded by Madame de Maintenon. It seems improbable that they undertook to make sets like this to order. Instead, St Aubin, in *L'Art du Brodeur*[9] asserts that convents of nuns undertook the working of *petit point* (tent stitch on canvas) for chair seats, which was regarded as too elementary (or perhaps too tedious) for professional workshops to undertake. These canvases, drawn out professionally, would be delivered with the silks to work them, and the payment would help to eke out the income of the convent.

The stories of Greece and Rome were known and enjoyed by those who had no knowledge of Latin or Greek. There are constant allusions to them in the plays of Shakespeare and in the works of other English writers and poets; and they did not need, as they do now, a footnote to explain them. Illustrated books, like those already mentioned, were popular, and even those who had not learned the Latin of Virgil knew of Aeneas, and the Wooden Horse that was the downfall of Troy, and the tragic love story of Dido, Queen of Carthage. It was for a performance in a girls' boarding school in Chelsea in 1689 that Henry Purcell wrote the haunting music of the first English opera *Dido and Aeneas*.

In 1659 a handsomely illustrated translation of the works of Virgil was published by John Ogilby (1600–1676). This enterprising man, neither printer nor bookseller, had been a dancing master, a tutor in private families and to Cambridge students, and Master of the King's Revels in Dublin. His splendid folios, still a joy to handle, were illustrated by such artists as Wenceslas Hollar and Franz Cleyn. Ogilby sold his volumes by the novel means of organising a lottery, the prizes being his books. Samuel Pepys won one, although Ogilby complained that those who did not draw prizes were reluctant to pay for their tickets. The full-page illustrations served as designs for the canvas work cover of an armchair now in the Victoria and Albert Museum. The back, cushion, wings, arms and seat all have scenes from the *Aeneid*, Virgil's history of Aeneas and the fall of Troy. Dido and Aeneas sit feasting on the back of the chair, while the legs of the Wooden Horse appear almost hidden beneath the cushion on the seat. Another illustration from the same volume is followed closely in a large hanging now at Montacute House, Somerset. It shows Venus appearing in the guise of a huntress before Aeneas and his faithful follower, Achates.

Virgil's *Georgics* (*Georgica*), a poem about agricultural pursuits, and almost as popular a schoolbook as his *Aeneid* was also published in translation by Ogilby, and illustrated by the same team of artists. Designs from this volume appear on a six-fold needlework screen[10] at Wallington, Northumberland, signed and dated *Julia Calverley 1727*. She was the daughter of Sir William Blackett, a mayor of Newcastle, and the wife of Sir Walter Calverley of Esholt, near Bradford. Sir Walter Calverley is said to have served as the model for Sir Roger de Coverley, a man of great good sense, who appeared in *The Spectator* of Richard Addison. Julia Calverley was a notable needlewoman. At Wallington, which her son inherited, there hang ten canvas work wall panels which she is recorded as having completed in three years. There are also six chairs with backs and seats in the same technique.[11]

It was, indeed, a needlework design taken from a classical and not a biblical source that was first identified as deriving from an engraving. This was in 1918, when the late C. E. C. Tattersall, of the Victoria and Albert Museum, first recognised that three figures on a large tent stitch hanging were taken from an engraving by Philip Galle (1537–1612).[12] (Plates 29–30.)

The hanging is one of the many richly complicated pictorial pieces belonging to the end of the sixteenth century. The figures wear the stiff costume fashionable in the French court of that period, and inevitably many of these hangings and valances

Plate 29. Coverlet. Centre panel: *Lucretia's Banquet*. Coloured wools and some silks on canvas. Tent stitch. The intended use of this piece is unknown: the corner heads suggest it was not a table carpet. Its size, the skilful arrangement of the borders within the strapwork, and its workmanship all suggest it was made in a professional workshop. Figures on the centre panel derive from an engraving by Philip Galle. Late 16th century. 167·5 × 297 cm. *Victoria and Albert Museum.*

have been optimistically attributed to the needle of Mary Queen of Scots during her long imprisonment, mainly on account of the costume. When this first identification was made by Tattersall it appeared to be a breakthrough, but it must be admitted that although after patient search other individual figures, like those of *Lucretia's Banquet*, have been found in engravings, yet many others, wearing these ornate court costumes, have so far defied any attempt to find their printed origins. Those that have been identified, however, suggest that they were drawn on to the canvas by pattern drawers who, as later, relied on a collection of prints for their figure drawing.

One such panel, which lacks the elegant court costume, but is in the same fine tent stitch and of even larger dimensions than *Lucretia's Banquet*, is at Scone Palace, Perthshire. It shows two allegorical female figures, representing Justice and Peace, embracing, with a verse in Latin from Psalm 85: 'Mercy and Truth are met together, righteousness and peace have kissed each other'. It is surrounded by a rich border filled with symbols of Righteousness (Divine justice) such as Jezebel being eaten by dogs, and the small boys who mocked Elisha's bald head being devoured by bears. The symbols of Peace include clasped hands, a young child leading the calf and the lion, and the wolf lying down with the lamb, all from the Old Testament. (Plate 31.)

Plate 30. Engraving *Lucretia's Banquet* by Philip Galle. Three figures (man, left foreground, man with wide moustache and the serving man with tankard) are copied on to the central panel of the coverlet. The figures of the women have been adapted, and wear more elaborate costumes than in the engraving.

In this case, the panel follows very closely an engraving published in Antwerp around 1574 (Plate 32) engraved by Jean Wierix who belonged to a family of engravers.[13] Even the symbols of the border are found on the print. The transferring of a panel from an engraving 33 × 44 cm. on to a panel so much larger (350 cm. wide: nearly eleven and a half feet) and of different proportions, would require a skilled pattern drawer. Its size alone suggests that it was made in a professional workshop. This assumption is strengthened by the fact that a similar panel, but with a different border of fruit and flowers instead of the austere symbolism of the engraving, appeared for sale on the London market after the first world war. Its present whereabouts are unknown.

It can be assumed therefore that just as the figures in needlework with Bible scenes were taken from woodcuts or engravings, so the goddesses and nymphs borrowed

Plate 31. Allegorical panel. Coloured wools and silks on canvas. Tent stitch. The Latin motto is from Psalm 85: *Mercy and Truth are met together, Righteousness and Peace have kissed each other*. Left: Righteousness (Divine Justice) with sword and scales flanked by Moses with the Tables of the Law. Right: Peace with an olive branch, the lance and shield of war being trodden on. Beyond: the Crucifixion. late 16th century. 350 cm. wide. *The Earl of Mansfield*.

Plate 32. Engraving *Righteousness and Peace embracing* by Hieronymus Wierix, after a
drawing by M. de Vos published in Antwerp about 1574 with a Latin verse by Hugo
Favolius. On the needlework panel the design has been extended at the sides by
additional landscape. The symbols of Peace and Divine Justice in the border are skilfully
reproduced in the textile. 33·5 × 44 cm. *Stadelijk Prentenkabinet, Antwerp.*

from classical mythology, and allegorical figures whose meaning sometimes now
eludes us, all came from printed sources and were transferred painstakingly on to the
linen, satin or canvas for the needlewoman to embroider.

References

1. Ovid: *Publius Ovidus Naso* (45 B.C. to A.D. 18) a Roman poet, whose elegant verse
   was studied and admired throughout the Middle Ages and Renaissance. An English
   translation of the *Metamorphoses* is available in Penguin Classics translated by Mary M.
   Innes.
2. For an assessment of the various illustrated editions of the *Metamorphoses* of Ovid from
   the 16th to the 17th centuries see: Henkel M. D. Illustrierte Ausgaben von Ovid's
   Metamorphosen im XV, XVI, XVII Jahrhundert, in Bibliothek Warburg, *Vorträge*
   1926–27 (Leipzig 1930).

3. Standen E. A Picture for every Story in *Metropolitan Museum of Art Bulletin* 1957 p. 161.
4. Musées Royaux d'Art et d'Histoire, Brussels No. TX. 1313. (Bequest Is. Errara).
5. Identified by John L. Nevinson. There are two needlework pictures deriving from the same engraver, both depicting the story of Atalanta and Meleager, in the Metropolitan Museum (gift of Judge Untermyer).
6. Now on loan to Aston Hall, Birmingham, See: Thorpe W. A. Stoneleigh Abbey and its furniture in the *Connoisseur* Dec. 1946 pp. 76 and 77. The engravings from which the designs are taken have not yet been located.
7. Basco J. The Splendour of Régence in *Rotunda* (Royal Ontario Museum Bulletin) Winter 1973 Vol. 6 no. 1 pp. 4–13.
8. Another chair deriving from *Metamorphoses en Rondeaux* is in the Metropolitan Museum (64.101.955) Source identified by Nancy Graves Cabot.
9. St Aubin M. *L'Art du Brodeur* L'Academie des Sciences Paris 1770.
10. One of the incidents on the screen from Virgil's *Eclogue* IX is found also on a needlework picture now in the Metropolitan Museum. Identified by Nancy Graves Cabot. See: Hackenbroch Y. *English and other Needlework . . . in the Irwin Untermyer Collection* 1960 Plate 126 fig. 166.
11. Wingfield Digby G. Lady Julia Calverley, Embroideress, in *Connoisseur* Vol. CXLV 1960 pp. 82 and 169.
12. Tattersall C. E. C. Mrs E. L. Franklin's Petit point Panel *Burlington Magazine* 1918 No. 890 Vol. CXIX pp. 343–4.

6

THE BEST ACTORS IN THE WORLD

Theatrical illustrations

Stories told aloud or read have engaged the imagination of mankind from time immemorial. Chaucer's pilgrims passed the time on their journey to Canterbury by telling each other stories: stories that have been read and re-read ever since. Stories from the Old and New Testaments: the patience of Job beneath his crushing misfortunes, and the tender humanity of the Good Samaritan, have all been absorbed into the language and thought of western civilisation.

More powerful than the written word, more powerful even than a live story teller, however beguiling, is the play. It is the theatrical story, where the characters are embodied in live human beings, displaying their griefs and joys in an enclosed space, the stage, through the invisible fourth wall of which we, the audience, can watch and listen to their tragedies and comedies. Even where there was no theatre, travelling players took this magic to the market towns of country districts, wherever there was an audience. In places too remote even for travelling players, country people mounted their own plays: nativity plays, miracle plays, from the great Passion Play still enacted every ten years at Oberammergau, to the humble village Mummers' play with its stock characters of St George and the Doctor.

Actors are soon forgotten, although by the time of Shakespeare great actors began to have a personal reputation, based on a part they played. During the following centuries woodcuts or engravings were made for sale, showing popular actors, actresses, singers and dancers in their best-known parts. In Paris towards the end of the seventeenth century many engravings were made and sold by such firms as Nicholas Bonnart and Jean Mariette showing popular stage figures. Some were drawn by Jean Bérain (1640–1711) the tapestry and stage designer. These prints offered delightfully decorative figures, some wearing stage headdresses of waving ostrich plumes, that could be used by pattern drawers of needlework.

One such print, published by Jean Mariette of the Rue St Jacques, Paris, shows an actor wearing a striped costume and a wide beret, standing on a stage, the boards of which are clearly visible. He was Angelo Constantini, a member of the Italian

Plate 33. Fire screen. Carved and gilded wood
with needlework panel. Coloured wools and
silks on canvas. The male figure derives from a
theatrical print. See Plate 34. About 1755.
96·5 × 61 cm. *Victoria and Albert Museum.*

Troupe established in Paris in 1688, playing the part of Mezzetino, a character in the
Italian Commedia dell'Arte. The same figure appears on a tent stitch fire screen, now
in the Victoria and Albert Museum. The stage boards have been transformed into a
flowery landscape, complete with sheep, dappled deer, a squirrel and flying birds.
The actor addresses himself to a seated lady with two pet dogs. (Plates 33 and 34.) The
ornate gilded frame of the screen follows very closely the design of the *Horse Fire
Screen* in *The Gentleman and Cabinetmaker's Director* published by Thomas
Chippendale in 1754.[1] Dancers and opera singers engraved by Mariette have been
found on needlework chair covers made in France and Italy.

Plate 34. Engraving. Angelo Constantini in the part of
Mezzetino, a character in the Italian *Commedia dell' Arte*.
Constantini was a member of the Italian troupe playing in
Paris in 1688. Jean Mariette, Paris. 30·5 × 19 cm. *The Pierpont
Morgan Library, New York*.

Mariette also published idealised portraits of members of the royal family of
France and other countries, as well as the nobility, the ladies wearing rich formal
gowns and high lace headdresses. The engravings are so clearly drawn that they have
been used as the basis of 'dressed prints', where the costume details are covered with
meticulously cut snippets of silk and velvet pasted on to the paper to give realism to
the portrait. Mariette and Nicholas Bonnart also published a series of female figures
representing the Months and the Seasons, perhaps as designs for stage or

masquerade costumes. Many of these appear on needlework firescreens and chair backs during the first half of the eighteenth century — proof of the popularity of these elegant, richly clad ladies.

Italian comedy, with the stock figures of Harlequin, Columbine, Punchinello and Pantaloon, was popular in France and Britain as well as its native Italy. Twelve long narrow needlework hangings, now in the Germanisches National Museum, Nuremberg, made in Dresden around 1711 and 1718,[2] were worked on canvas in tent and cross stitch. The central figure on each panel comes from Italian comedy, the designs are from known theatrical prints. Two other comedians on the panels can be traced to designs by Bérain.

The figure of Harlequin appears in the most unexpected places. An English armchair, whose back is decorated with the surprising scene from the New Testament of the apostle Philip baptising the Eunuch of Ethiopia, whom he encountered reading the prophesy of Isaiah while being driven through the desert,[3] has apparently unrelated figures on the wings and arms. There is an elegant shepherdess with attendant gentleman, an oriental potentate, and the figure of Harlequin. The same figure appears on one of the panels of the screen embroidered and signed by Lady Julia Calverley (see p. 60). Both Harlequins derive from the same French theatrical print, published by Bonnart. (Plates 35 and 36.) The pattern drawer of Lady Julia Calverley's screen drew upon the illustrations from Ogilby's *Virgil* and from a theatrical print; whoever drew the designs on the chair seat had an even wider selection of prints to follow, and did not appear to find it incongruous to mix them freely.

Popular prints of plays and players were widely used as patterns for ceramic figures in most of the porcelain manufactories in the eighteenth century, and a great deal of research has uncovered the sources of these delightful examples of the modeller's art. Meissen, Chelsea and Bow all produced theatrical figures, characters from the *Commedia dell' Arte* and portraits of actors in well-known roles. In 1740 David Garrick's mythological burlesque *Lethe* was performed at Drury Lane Theatre. Ten years later, the Bow factory reproduced in porcelain two actors as characters in the play: Kitty Clive, who played the part of The Fine Lady, and Henry Woodward. Both were modelled after prints published in 1750.

Prints illustrating scenes from the plays of Shakespeare were published in London by John and Josiah Boydell between 1789 and 1803. They were very popular as patterns for needlework pictures executed with great skill at schools for young ladies in New England.[5] They were, perhaps, intended more as illustrations of tales from Shakespeare rather than scenes of an actual performances on the stage. (Plates 37 and 38.)

In Britain, theatrical prints achieved their widest popularity in the nineteenth century. These were the 'penny plain, twopence coloured' prints, produced by small family firms, such as J. K. Green, who claimed to have been in 1808 'the original inventor and publisher of Juvenile Theatrical Prints'. His plates were bought in 1860 by a jobbing printer with a shop in Hoxton named John Redington, whose daughter

Plate 35. Detail from a six-fold needlework screen, worked by
Lady Julia Calverley and dated 1727. Coloured wools on
canvas. Tent stitch. Some of the other panels show scenes
from the illustrations in Ogilby's volume of the works of Virgil
published 1654. For Harlequin see Plate 36, the other figures
unidentified. Wallington Hall, Northumberland. *The National
Trust for England and Wales.*

Eliza married Benjamin Pollock, a furrier. She persuaded Pollock to take over the
business, and today his name is the only one remembered as the printer of the
Victorian toy theatre, one of the delights of Robert Louis Stevenson and many
another Victorian child.

Redington's shop sold toy theatres and the miniature figures that could be cut
out and held on wires on the stage, together with the playbook and scenery. In

Plate 36. Engraving *Harlequin*. A theatrical print published by
Nicholas Bonnart, Paris. *The Pierpont Morgan Library, New
York.*

addition, he and the other publishers of toy theatres, sold full size theatrical portraits
(6½ by 8½ inches) that could be bought for 'tinselling', together with sheets of tinsel
ornaments to decorate the figures of the actors striking dramatic poses: tiny tinsel
crowns, swords and breastplates. These were stuck on in the manner of scraps, to
make brightly coloured flamboyant pictures, usually the hobby of young boys, like
the toy theatres. They are, in fact, Victorian versions of the 'dressed print' of the
seventeenth century.[6] It was John Redington who introduced the use of lithography,
printing on stone, which reduced the cost of printing. The prints were widely

Plate 37. Stipple engraving *Cymbeline* by Thomas Burke after a painting by William
Hamilton, published in 1795 by John and Josiah Boydell, London. 43 × 58·5 cm.
Old Sturbridge Village, Massachusetts.

distributed, and as with the figures of Bow and Chelsea, so the Staffordshire potters
began to manufacture figures of popular actors, using these prints as models.[7]

The 'penny plain, twopence coloured' prints of actors also served as models for a
curious type of patchwork executed with superlative skill by men around the middle
of the nineteenth century. Small pieces of woollen cloth, broadcloth, frieze and
tweed, clippings from tailors' workrooms, were made into patchwork bedcovers and
tablecloths. It appears to have been done entirely as a hobby, often as occupational
therapy in military and naval hospitals, using snippets of uniform material, and
often, of necessity, the patches are extremely small. Some of the most remarkable,
however, are made by tailors. They show figures of Crimean generals, the royal
family or actors, all executed in inlaid patchwork, where the shape has been cut out
and cloth of the same shape but a different colour has been skilfully inserted, the
edges oversewn. It is, indeed, a fabric version of the art of marquetry in wood, except
that the cloth is not stuck down to the foundation, and unlike wood, the cut edges can
fray unless they are neatly and firmly sewn to the surrounding material. It can be
seen therefore, that a high degree of skill in cutting and sewing is required to depict

Plate 38. Needlework picture. *Cymbeline wrought by Ann Trask at Mrs. Rowson's Academy*. Silk embroidery on silk with painted details. Ann Trask (born 1795) was one of three sisters who attended Susanna Rowson's Academy in Boston. Silk needlework pictures, worked to a very high standard and taken from a variety of prints, were exceedingly popular subjects at schools for young ladies in New England at the end of the 18th and the beginning of the 19th centuries. 43 × 58 cm. *Old Sturbridge Village, Massachusetts*.

lively figures in uniform or stage costume. It would appear that the print was cut up and the various shapes used as templates for the meticulously cut cloth.

In Scotland, several examples of this exacting technique survive. Two of the most remarkable are preserved at the Town House, Biggar, worked by a local tailor, Menzies Moffat (1829–1907), who described himself as master tailor, artist and photographer.[8] He was an eccentric and a recluse, regarded as something of a joke by his fellow townsmen, and tormented by the local small boys. He was, however, a competent photographer to judge by his surviving *carte de visite* portraits. He called the larger panel *The Royal Crimean Hero Tablecover*, borrowing the name of a well-known pattern of damask table-linen woven at Dunfermline. It has equestrian figures of the main Crimean leaders in the border: Lord Raglan, Omar Pasha, Sir Lacey Evans and Marechal Pelissier. The central panel has medallions of Queen

Victoria and the Prince Consort, surrounded by ladies of the court, as yet unidentified. Around are rectangles of theatrical figures: Punchinello, Columbine, General Tom Thumb, Mr Payne as *Robin Hood* and Mr King as *Little John* from a Redington print. There is also a spirited representation in cloth of a print published by M. and M. Skelt (flourished 1837–40) entitled *St Andrew and the Winged Serpent. No. 14 Horses Price Halfpenny*. In all, Menzies Moffat's tablecover comprises figures from 81 prints. The scraps of coloured cloth, all woollen, have been joined with great skill. There are

Plate 39. Coverlet inscribed *Executed by David Robertson Falkirk Stirlingshire N.B. in 1650 Hours. 1853*. Broadcloth and other woollen fabrics. Inlaid patchwork. Chain and other stitches in silk. The figures derive from theatrical and popular prints. David Robertson was a tailor, and the cloth is probably tailors' clippings. *Glasgow Art Gallery and Museum.*

narrow borders of contrasting material embellished with a delicate tracery of motives, flowers, stars and arabesques, embroidered in silk using mainly tailors' stitches: herringbone, buttonhole, back stitch and interlaced running stitch.

Moffat wrote the story of his life in a wallpaper pattern book, which has, alas, been destroyed. The Tablecover only survived by an accident. It was his last wish that he should be buried in it, but this was denied him, no doubt because it was considered another of his eccentricities, and unseemly for one buried by the parish.

Plate 40. Detail of Plate 39. The coloured patches are cut out from contrasting cloth and inserted, not applied to the background. The faces are embroidered.

N° 33 *Horse*.   GENERAL SIR ROBERT SALE.

Plate 41. Popular print *General Sir Robert Sale* published by A. Park
(1818–1880) London. No. 33 in the series *Horses*. Major-General Sir
Robert Sale (1782–1845), hero of the Afghan War, was nicknamed
'Fighting Bob'. These prints were sold for tinselling: scraps of tinsel
to represent horse-trappings, and silks were stuck on to decorate the
prints. It was a popular pastime for young boys in the mid-19th century
and flourished alongside the Victorian Toy Theatre. 25 × 20 cm.
The Museum of London.

MR DUCROW AS HARLEQUIN.

London, Pub. June 10th 1830, by R. LLOYD, Dramatic Repository, 40 Gibson St near the Coburg Theatre.

Plate 42. Theatrical print *Mr. Ducrow as Harlequin.* Published by R. Lloyd (flourished 1828–33) London 1830. Andrew Ducrow (1793–1842) was a renowned equestrian performer and popular with William IV. A print sold for tinselling. The figures and horse-trappings were sometimes cut out and used as templates for the silk and tinsel: the remainder painted with water colour. The horse has been omitted from David Robertson's patchwork (Plate 40). 22 × 31 cm. *The Museum of London.*

Other tailors made these covers of inlaid pictorial patchwork. Several survive in Wales.[9] John Munro, a tailor, the self-styled Paisley Artist, born 1811, worked an elaborate panel called *The Royal Clothograph Work of Art* which took eighteen years to complete. There are seven scenes, each surrounded by geometrical pieced borders. One reproduces the stalwart nautical figure of Mr T. P. Cooke from a Skelt print as *William in Black Ey'd Susan.* The patchwork version is captioned *Britain for Ever.*

Another Scottish tailor, like Menzies Moffat, completed two covers. One, dated 1853, is inscribed *Executed by David Robertson Falkirk Stirlingshire N.B. in 1650 hours.* (Plate 39.) The central panel displays a fully rigged ship with the Royal Arms above. Around it are panels taken from tinsel prints: *Mr Gomersal as Napoleon*

Bounaparte and *General Sir Robert Sale* both in the *Horses* series, and *Mr Ducrow as Harlequin* published in 1830 by R. Lloyd. (Plates 40, 41, and 42.)

Engravings of popular actors and actresses in favourite roles have scarcely been considered as the probable source of pictorial needlework, in spite of the research that has shown how much they were used as patterns for the makers of porcelain in the eighteenth century. It could be that the fine ladies with their attendant gentlemen that appear on embroidered screens and chair covers may be portraits of actors and actresses.

References

1. Identified by Nancy Graves Cabot.
2. Schuette, M. and Muller-Christensen, S. *Das Stickereiwerk* Tübingen 1963 Plate XXVII and Figure 429. Wilckens, L. v. 'Zwolf gestichte Wandebehänge aus Dresden' in *Pantheon International Zeitschrift für Kunst* XX 1962 Heft 2 pp. 69–76.
3. In the Metropolitan Museum, (64.101.913). Illustrated in Hackenbroch, Y. *English and other Needlework in the Untermyer Collection* London 1960 figs. 70, 71. The New Testament incident (Acts VIII 26–39) portrayed derives from no. 111 in *History of the Old and New Testament described in figures* published by Samuel Keble at the Turks Head Fleet Street (London) 1694, but the illustration is itself taken mainly from Matthew Merian's New Testament published in Frankfurt in 1627.
4. See various issues of the *Transactions* of the English Ceramic Circle.
5. Nylander, J. C. Some print sources of New England Schoolgirl art. *Antiques* Vol. CX no. 2 Aug. 1976 p. 295.
6. For a full account of these prints and their publishers, see Speaight, G. *The History of the English Toy Theatre* Studio Vista 1969.
7. Hall, J. *Staffordshire Figures*. Charles Letts & Co. 1972.
8. I am indebted to Mr Brian Lambie, founder of Gladstone Court Museum of Biggar, Lanarkshire for the biographical details relating to Menzies Moffat. There is an octagonal panel, called by Moffat *The Star Table Cover* showing various scenes, also preserved at the Town House.
9. Anthony, I. E. 'Quilting and Patchwork in Wales' in *Amgueddfa*, Bulletin of the National Museum of Wales. No. 12 Winter 1972. The technique was also practised in the United States. A woollen cover worked in inlaid patchwork is in the Abby Aldrich Rockefeller Folk Art Collection, Williamsburg, Va. (74.603.1) but the design is floral, and unlike the British examples does not derive from a popular print.

7

SOME CUNNING WORKES

Printed pattern books for embroiderers

Illustrations from a surprising variety of books have been pressed into service as models by the domestic and professional embroiderer. They include books of natural history, herbals, books of flora and fauna, native and exotic, emblem books, illustrated Bibles, the classics and mythology, illustrations of novels and plays.

Some books were also published specifically for embroiderers. Of these, only a few copies survive, mainly because, if they were at all popular or useful, the pages were cut out, or pricked through, so that they suffered considerably harder wear than books intended merely to be read. Amongst the earliest is a volume published by Peter Quentel in Cologne in 1527. Like the Cologne Bible, the woodcuts set a style followed with variations by other publishers, in Italy, France and England. The designs are sometimes linear, as if for braiding, sometimes for what was then called *Spanish Stitch* (double running or Holbein stitch), often on squared paper for darned net, or *Lacis*, and some are for other laces such as the geometrical cutwork worked on a linen or thread foundation. As happened with the Bible illustrations, publishers freely borrowed or copied designs from other publications.[1]

It would be wrong to assume that these books were published for any domestic needlewoman living remote from pattern drawers. The well-known *Singuliers et nouveaux pourtraicts* of 1587 by the Venetian, Frederigo Vinciolo, and dedicated to the Dowager Queen of France, Catherine de Medici[2] was embellished by a sonnet 'aux Dames et Demoiselles' urging them to use the patterns in the book, and to master the craft of *Lacis*. Those likely to buy these books were not simple countrywomen, but ladies like Catherine de Medici and Bess of Hardwick; ladies who had in their households a professional embroiderer, or someone able to draw out the designs for them to work.

The first pattern book published in English appears to be W. Vosterman's *A neawe treatys as concerning the excellency of the nedle worke spannisshe stitches and weaving in the frame* published about 1530 in Antwerp. This is a version of Quentel's pattern book, and only one copy is known: that in the Arsenal Library, Paris. Equally rare is *Morysse and Damashin renewed and encreased Very profitable for Goldsmythes and Embroiderers by Thomas Geminus at London Anno 1548*, a tiny book about two and a half by three and a half inches (6.5 ×9 cm). Geminus was a Flemish surgeon and instrument maker employed at the Court. The only known copy of his book is preserved at the Landesmuseum Münster, Germany. It shows designs for strapwork appliqué, more useful to the professional embroiderer than the domestic needlewoman.

In 1586 there followed *La Clef des Champs* published in Blackfriars, London and dedicated to Lady Mary Sidney. Here we are on more familiar ground, for the book contains 98 sensitive but useful woodcuts of flowers, fruit (the fashionable peapod) and animals, some of the latter borrowed from Gesner, all of them motives beloved by the Elizabethan and Stuart domestic needlewoman. They have captions in English, French, German and Latin.

The author, Jacques le Moyne de Morgue, was a French protestant, a native of Dieppe, who had visited Florida in 1564, and escaped to England from France after the massacre of St Bartholomew's Day in 1572. He settled in Blackfriars and died in 1588. His watercolour drawings of flowers and some of his American sketches are preserved in the British Museum and the Victoria and Albert Museum, and show him as a sensitive and observant draughtsman. The delicate woodcuts of *La Clef des Champs*, intended for the use of goldsmiths, embroiderers and tapestry designers, show clear and simple shapes, admirably suited to their purpose. They include the familiar daisy, pink or carnation, honeysuckle (woodbine) pansy (*Pawnsie*: French *Pensée*) wild rose (Eglantine) and the popular peapod. The outlines of many of these in the two copies now in the British Museum are pricked, demonstrating the use to which the books were put. So far, however, no embroideries have been identified as deriving from *La Clef des Champs*.

English publishers were not slow to borrow from tested and tried continental publications. In 1591 A. Poyntz issued *New and singular pattern and workes of linen*, which despite its title was a copy of Vinciolo's *Les singuliers et nouveaux pourtraicts* of 1587, while W. Bailey in *A Booke of Curious and strange Inventions* 1596 copied the designs in an Italian book published by G. Ciotti five years earlier. Even the well-known and often quoted *The Needles' Excellency*, published by James Boler at the Sign of the Marigold in St Paul's Churchyard (10th edition 1634), with its title page inscribed 'Newly invented and cut in copper for the pleasure and profit of the Industrious' had copied the designs from various editions of Sibmacher's *Mödelbuch*, the first of which had appeared in 1597 in Nuremberg. It is chiefly remembered for its poem by John Taylor, the Water Poet, with its list of stitches, and poems in praise of famous needlewomen. Indeed, it seems unlikely that Taylor ever saw the book before the wrote his verses:

> And as this booke some cunning workes doth teach,
> (Too hard for meane capacities to reach)
> So for weake learners, other workes here be,
> As plaine and easie as are A B C.
> Thus skilfull, or unskillfull, each may take,
> This booke, and of it, each good use may make,
> All sorts of workes, almost than can be name'd,
> Here are directions how they may be fram'd:

Plate 43. Line designs from *The Scholehouse of the Needle* published by Richard Shorleyker, London. Two known surviving copies are dated 1624 and 1632, and may be later editions of a popular book. Sprigs such as these are common on shirts and caps of the period.

If we except *La Clef des Champs* as designed by a Frenchman, though published in London, the only early English pattern book that has any claim to be a native product is Richard Shorleyker's *A scholehouse for the needle*. The two remaining copies are dated 1624 and 1632, but earlier editions may have been published. Even here some of the lace patterns are borrowed from Sibmacher and Vinciolo. The title page offers 'sundry sorts of spots, as Flowers, Birds and Fishes &c. and will fitly serve to be wrought, some with Gould, some with Silke and some with Crewell, or otherwise at your pleasure'. The only two known copies, in the Victoria and Albert Museum, and in the Bodleian Library, Oxford, are both incomplete. They show flowers, birds and animals arranged in rows, clearly printed for the needlewoman to follow. Plate 43.

John Nevinson has found two of Shorleyker's designs, birds on flowery branches, on an almost contemporary sampler in the collection of the Victoria and Albert Museum.[3] Apart from that, these early pattern books are disappointing fields for search and tell us little of the needs and techniques of the domestic needlewoman of the period. Most of the pattern books, it is true, offer designs for lace, filet or

Plate 44. White linen sampler, in
horizontal bands of cut and drawn
thread work, inscribed at top M P
1667. Two designs, second and
fourth row from the top, are from
Sibmacher (See Plate 45). 89·5 ×
18 cm. *The Royal Scottish Museum.*

Plate 45. Design for cutwork, netting or cross stitch, counted on squares, from Johann Sibmacher *Neues Modelbuch in Kupfer gemacht*, Nuremberg 1601, a popular pattern book that ran to several editions, and was copied by English publishers.

cutwork, that may have been made in large quantities to wear, but which could have disintegrated in the succeeding years. Samplers containing lace stitch bands have been preserved, and three at least show that Sibmacher's *Schön neues Mödelbuch* of 1597 was followed, either in the original, or in a pirated edition.[4] (Plates 44 and 45).

Shorleyker's designs are very close to those worked in red, blue or black thread on the few linen shirts or shifts that have survived, and we should bear in mind that much needlework made for costume, as well as for furnishing, has disappeared over the centuries; all we are left with is a tiny fraction of the domestic output.

A perfect title for a book of needlework designs could have been *The Ladies Amusement* published in 1758–62 by Robert Sayer, Print and Map Seller at the Golden Buck, Fleet Street, London. It was, alas, subtitled *The Whole Art of Japanning made easy*, and it comprised two hundred pages of elegantly drawn designs of *Flowers, Shells, Insects, Landscapes, Shipping, Beasts, Vases, borders, etc.*, many of them Chinoiserie designs drawn by the French artist Jean Pillement (1719–1808). Although this has been proved to be a bountiful source of inspiration to designers of japanned furniture, printed cottons, enamels and porcelain, so far no needlework has been traced to its design. The amusement it afforded does not appear to have included embroidery.[5]

When the *Lady's Magazine* began to publish embroidery designs in 1770, these also were intended mostly for dress. It is rare to find a volume complete with its inset pattern; it is equally rare, if not impossible, to find a ruffle or kerchief known to be from the magazine. Even nearer to our own time, *The Englishwoman's Domestic Magazine* published by Samuel Beaton, who also published his famous wife's *Household Management*, included folded plates of coloured needlework patterns between 1861 and 1864. The patterns were often torn out of the bound volumes, so it must be assumed that they were frequently used, yet it is difficult to find one that can be traced to this popular journal. Pattern books for needlework, it would seem, were eagerly used, but the resulting embroidery has been lost to us.

References

1. Lotz A. *Bibliographie der Modelbucher* Leipzig 1933.
   Abegg M. *Apropos Patterns* Zurich 1978.
2. Now published in facsimile by Dover Publications Inc. For a list of English pattern books see: Nevinson J. L. *Catalogue of English Domestic Embroidery*. Victoria and Albert Museum 1938 p. XXV.
3. V. and A. (T279–1923). Nevinson J. L. English Domestic Embroidery Patterns of the Sixteenth and Seventeenth Centuries in *Walpole Society* Vol. XXVIII (1939–40).
4. Royal Scottish Museum (1931.61) Dated 1667. Victoria and Albert Museum (T291–1916) Dated 1729. Fitzwilliam Museum, Cambridge (T20.1938) Undated.
5. *The Ladies Amusement or the whole art of Japanning made easy* printed for Robert Sayer. Facsimile edition. Ceramic Book Company Newport, Mon. 1966.

8

DRAWING OF A MUCHNESS

Manuscripts and manuscript books of patterns

The printed page offered many delightful patterns for needlework, intentionally or unintentionally. There are also manuscripts that survive to supplement what could not be found in the books available, and so widen the choice, especially for the domestic needlewoman, if she found herself far from the professional pattern drawer. It must be assumed that every pattern drawer had himself a collection of sheets with the designs drawn out to a suitable size and shape: even pricked ready for use, but so far no such collection has come to light.

A manuscript book dated 1608 bound into two volumes containing many embroidery designs is now in the Folger Shakespeare Library, Washington., D.C.[1] It was compiled by Thomas Trevelyon, born about 1548, who was probably buried in the parish of St Bride's, Fleet Street on 18 August 1627 during an epidemic of the plague. Apart from his self-portrait in the book, which shows him as a serious, bearded, stocky figure carrying a book and wearing a long furred black gown with a ruff and a black hat with a round crown, we know tantalisingly little about him. In spite of intensive research by John Nevinson, who suggests that he was a writing master, and may have worked in a shop in London, no further details have as yet come to light.

The patterns in the books are by no means only for needlework; indeed, the embroidery patterns are only to be found after scriveners' alphabets, drawings, allegories, transcripts from herbals and from Topsell's *Historie of Foure-Footed Beasts*. The embroidery patterns are simply listed as 'drawne works' in the index, and although they could have been used for other purposes, wood carving or plaster work, they are very similar to the surviving embroideries of the period, especially those that appear on linen coifs, sleeves and cushions. Some are so close that one searches in vain for the same motif on existing embroideries and samplers. That they were intended for embroiderers is without question. There is a series showing designs for men's caps to be made up in four sections, some with a matching design for the turned-up brim. It is the type of cap made with four or more sections, that remained fashionable as informal wear for gentlemen at home until well into the eighteenth century, as long as the fashion for wearing wigs continued. Caps of this shape embroidered in silk, metal thread, worsted, or white quilting have survived, but none, so far, has been found to correspond with Trevelyon's designs.

It may be that other manuscript designs still remain hidden in the libraries of private houses. One such, on loan to the National Library of Scotland, consists of some 162 designs on odd sheets of paper, some with accounts or messages written on their backs. They come from three different houses, but belong to a single family. The earliest and liveliest designs were worked under the direction of the family governess, a tiny scheming character called Henrietta Cumming, born in Edinburgh about 1734. Her father was a writing master (as Thomas Trevelyon is thought to have been). Her brother, James Cumming, was apprenticed to the Nories, a family of decorative painters in Edinburgh, and became a Herald Painter to the court of the Lord Lyon, the College of Heralds in Scotland. Henrietta's aunt Mrs Dallas with whom she first lived, belonged to a family of professional embroiderers in Edinburgh. Helen Dallas, her cousin, supplied the embroidered hangings for a mahogany bed sold to the Duke of Atholl in 1755 by the Edinburgh upholsterer, Schaw.[2]

Henrietta had a talent for drawing and had attended a school in Edinburgh. In 1760 she became governess to the family of the 5th Earl of Balcarres in Fife, and rapidly made herself indispensable to Lady Balcarres, who came to rely on her, not only to discipline her high-spirited and intelligent family of eight children, but also to undertake shopping and other commissions. She also had to chaperone the two elder girls, Lady Margaret and Lady Anne Lindsay (the author of the ballad *Auld Robin Gray*) on their visits to Edinburgh. They were friends of Sir Walter Scott and of David Hume, and moved in the circle of cultivated society of the period that gave Edinburgh the title of 'The Athens of the North'.[3]

In her efforts to ensure the girls were suitably though economically dressed, Lady Balcarres insisted that her daughters made some of their own finery, and they displayed a great deal of ingenuity in doing so. It is said that on one occasion they appeared at a soirée wearing curls of wood from a carpenter's plane decorating their hair. Henrietta wrote to her sister-in-law, the wife of James Cumming the painter: 'The Lady Bal: begs you would tell her what kind of bones is fit to make the everlasting white for painting gauze as she is determined her young ladies shall wear no other lappets but of their own painting.'[4]

The manuscript patterns show that many of the designs for lappets, fichus and ruffles, drawn out by Henrietta and the girls, were used for embroidery, and were by no means essays in drawing. Many are stitched around the edges, where the muslin has been tacked over the inked design. In the breathless unpunctuated letters sent by Lady Balcarres to 'Henny' while she was in Edinburgh are requests for threads and materials:

> ... When you send the ruffels lett me have cotton along with them as I have not one thread a little fine for the open [work?] the other between a shilling and eighteenpence as you see fitt if they come within this three weeks I shall not find fault at all your cusine send out other thre yeards pink nanky for a [petty?] for Willie I can not recollect anything further I have to say just now . . .[5]

Plate 46. Lower end of a manuscript design for a lappet. Ink on paper drawn by Henrietta Cumming (1734–1823), governess to the family of the 5th Earl of Balcarres. On the reverse is inscribed: *this is the lapet and cap which I think vastly pretty*. The edges of the paper have needleholes where the muslin for working was attached. 1761. 22·5 × 8·5 cm. *On loan to the National Library of Scotland.*

One well-drawn pattern on two sheets of paper is for a cap and lappet, the *barbe* or streamer of a cap, sometimes tied under the chin. It shows a charming rococo design suitable for drawn muslin or *Dresden work* (Plates 46 and 47) and is inscribed on the back in Henrietta's hand: 'this is the lapet and cap which I think vastly pretty'. (Plate 48).

Even the boys in the schoolroom were pressed into drawing out designs suitable for needlework. In the same collection, some of the patterns come from

Muncaster Castle, Cumbria. One, a simple all-over design of serpentine lines and dots for muslin is signed in a childish hand *John Pennington, Muncaster*. He was John, 1st Baron Muncaster (1740–1815). From the same source is a watercolour drawing of a design with a Greek key border and black ground with roundels containing moss roses and morning glories. It is signed in the same childish hand: *Copy of a Carpett*. Lying among these patterns is a printed design inscribed *Engraved for the Lady's Magazine*: a deep border of small sprigs and scallops, taken from one of the copies of this journal, which are still to be found in the family library.

Despite such a wealth of needlework patterns, drawn out and used, as the stitched edges of many testify, no single piece has survived as evidence of the skill of these family needlewomen. They were all made, worn, used and laundered until they disintegrated, or were just thrown out as old fashioned.

Some of the sheets show the delicate circular wreaths of tiny flowers and barley sprays that suggest the first two decades of the nineteenth century, and are signed *Harriet Wright*, who married Lord Overstone in 1829. They resemble the patterns that are to be found in many of the manuscript books that survive from this period. So many have come to light that it would appear to have been as fashionable for any young woman to collect needlework designs, as it was to compile a book of receipts. Like the receipt for a special dish, given by a friend, so a design sometimes bears the name of the donor. Harriet Wright, for instance, inscribes on the back of one sheet 'Miss Pyndar's patterns', and on two borders: 'Given me by Lady Caroline Bentinck'.

Although so many manuscript pattern books of this period have survived, only one has been published in facsimile to show the style and variety of these needlework patterns. It is now in the Valentine Museum, Richmond, Virginia, and is thought to be American, though the original compiler gave no clue to her identity.[6] The paper of the hand-made book has an English watermark of 1801. The designs comprise borders, sprays, handkerchief corners and deeper borders, one inscribed *The bottom of a Frock or Dress* suggesting the fashions of 1810 to 1820.

A book of the same period, in Strangers' Hall Museum, Norwich, is labelled simply *Pattern Book* and has around a thousand designs in it, of which 124 were cut or drawn from the *Lady's Magazine*. Some fifty sheets of these are signed Sophia Hase. She belonged to a Norfolk family and married Robert Marsham, who was High Sheriff of Norfolk in 1801. She died in 1824.[7]

Two more manuscript books of the period are in the National Library of Scotland. The leather binding of one is stamped *Miss Montgomery* and the elegant designs are drawn in ink and lightly filled in with sepia water colour on paper with the watermark *Whatman 1808*. It belonged to Barbara Montgomery who married Alexander Walker of Bowden near Galashiels in 1811.[8] The other is inscribed *Charlotte Scott from Sarah Eliza Jessop Decr. 8 1831* and is in an exercise book of plain paper. Compared with Miss Montgomery's book, it is a more humble production with 35 pages of embroidery pattern and two knitting patterns. At the back of the book, in reverse, are more knitting patterns and useful household receipts for such items as

Plate 47. Lower end of a lappet (the streamer or *barbe* of a cap), one of a pair. Drawn muslin or Dresden work, with a variety of fillings. Henrietta Cumming's design would have been worked in a similar technique. About 13 × 8 cm. *The Royal Scottish Museum.*

Plate 48. Border design with a corner. Ink on paper. Reverse: *Mar. L—y* and childish scribbles. Lady Margaret Lindsay (1752–1814) was the second daughter of the 5th Earl of Balcarres. Perhaps intended for the border of a gown. *c.* 1765. 106 × 32 cm. *On loan to the National Library of Scotland.*

Plate 49. Page from an anonymous manuscript book of designs. Scottish, about 1820. 22·5 × 18 cm.

pomatum, ointment and the reviving of gilt frames. (Plate 49.)

At least five others are known in private collections, all with a Scottish provenance, that can be dated between 1808 and 1837, and others are known to exist.[9] They show no evidence of use; instead, they remain like autograph books, reflections of the taste of their time, and are touching souvenirs of their owners. It must be charitably assumed that, when a design was selected from the book, it was traced off on to stouter paper for actual use.

Manuscript patterns, especially for white work, appear to have been collected just as assiduously in the United States at this period, but they seem to have been well employed. At Sturbridge Old Village, Massachusetts, there is a collection from several sources, many of them stitched around the edges. One, a baby's bonnet crown with a rosebud design, still has its circle of hemmed muslin waiting to be worked. Two others are inscribed *A New Pattern for working a Gown, etc. S. Welch 1791*, and *Device for an Embroider'd pocket Book S. Welch 1791*. The rest are anonymous, some of them drawn on the backs of pages from copy books, bearing, in copperplate handwriting such edifying maxims as 'Never countenance immorality but admonish with candour' repeated in unwavering lines to the foot of the page, with a somewhat worldly collar design on the reverse.[10]

A book of manuscript designs, compiled, not by a young lady before her marriage, but by a professional embroiderer and her daughter, survives from the late 1850s. It was intended as a book of sample edgings and monograms. Initials suitable for handkerchiefs are marked *6 Pence*; smaller and plainer are *3 Pence*, while some monograms have the name of the customer for whom they were devised: *Lady Murray, Lady Dalrymple Elphinstone*. Flowery names encountered on the large sheet of Victorian handkerchiefs are drawn out: *Julia, Jeanne, Mina, Henriette*. They were probably drawn out by Agnes Quintin Dalrymple, whose aunts and mother from 1834 to 1876 had a business in Edinburgh of embroiderers, dressmakers and milliners. For the last ten years, the firm was described as *Embroiderer, Lace mender and Transferer*.[11] No doubt every firm of embroiderers had similar sample books, supplemented by worked examples of their wares, from which a choice could be made.

References

1. Nevinson J. L. The Embroidery Patterns of Thomas Trevelyon *Walpole Society* Vol. XLI 1968. Trevelyon compiled a second book in 1616, now in a private collection in the United States. Many of the patterns are repeated in this volume.
2. Bamford F. The Schaws of Edinburgh and a bed at Blair Castle in *Furniture History* Vol. X 1974 p. 15.
3. Swain M. A wild kind of imagination, Embroidery pattern drawers 1760–1830 in *Country Life* January 26 1978 pp. 190–192.
4. Edinburgh University Library Laing MS 81/9.
5. Ed. Univ. Lib. Laing MS 81/3 Lady Balcarres to H.C. at Lady Dalrymple's.
6. Davis M. J. (ed. by) *Embroidery Designs 1780–1820* The Valentine Museum.
7. Clabburn P. A Norwich Pattern Book in *Embroidery* Summer 1970 pp. 56–57. See also *op. cit.* Autumn 1970 p. 88 for the book's owner.
8. National Library of Scotland 1. Walker of Bowden MS 184.d.127 2. MS 10388.
9. Hawkes G. M. Old Manuscript Pattern Books in the *Embroideress* No. 13 pp. 300–304.
10. Sturbridge Old Village: Collection 22.12.6 C/XXVI.
11. I am indebted to Mrs Mittell for allowing me to examine this MS sample book.

9
PREPARED PACKS

The prepared pack, or kit, is not quite such a modern marketing idea as we are led to believe. The polythene bag enclosing it may be new, but the contents—the design ready traced on the cloth, complete with sufficient thread in the necessary colours—have filled a need for much longer than many people are aware. It has always been necessary for those living in the country, far from the shops, to have to order materials and threads from a distance, and there is a real fear that the amount of thread, silk, or yarn, may be insufficient to complete the design. Husbands and sons were often charged with strict instructions regarding the purchase of embroidery materials. Mary Queen of Scots was obliged to write to the French Ambassador in London for supplies of embroidery silks during her enforced stay at Sheffield Castle. The drawing out of the designs offered no problem, as that was done for her by her embroiderer, but other needlewomen without a skilled assistant required an up-to-date design as well as sufficient cloth and the necessary threads.

In March 1687 Samuel Sewell of Boston, Massachusetts, wrote to Daniel Allen in London:

> I have two small daughters who begin to goe to school: my wife would intreat your good Lady to pleasure her so far as to by for her, white fustian drawn, enough for curtins, wallen [valance] counterpaine for a bed, and half a doz. chairs with four threeded green worsted to work it.[1]

The thick green worsted crewel wool in sufficient quantity to work the design, together with the traced fustian to make bed hangings and chair covers must have made a considerable pack to despatch overseas, and must have occupied the young girls and their mother for some months.

There is other evidence that bed hangings were obtainable in London ready drawn at this period. A set of bed hangings in Colonial Williamsburg, a bed curtain in the Museum of Fine Arts Boston (61.1250) and a curtain in the Victoria and Albert Museum (T390–1904) all bear the same drawn design, though the stitches and execution vary.[2]

Citizens of Boston were not obliged for long to send off for needlework supplies to London. By 1738 Mrs Condy was advertising in the *Boston News Letter*:

To be had at Mrs Condy's near the Old North Meeting House: All sorts of beautiful figures on Canvas, for Tent Stick; the Patterns from London, but drawn by her much cheaper than English drawing; All sorts of Canvas, without drawing; also Silk Shades, Slacks, Floss, Cruells of all Sorts, the best White Chapple Needles, and every thing for all Sorts of Work.[3]

Mrs Condy also taught needlework, as her advertisement of 1742 makes plain:

Persons may be supply'd with the Materials for the Work she teaches, whether they learn of her or not. She draws patterns of all sorts, especially, Pocket-Books, House-Wives, Screens, Pictures, Chimney-pieces, Escrutoires, etc. for Tent-Stitch, in a plainer Manner, and cheaper than those which come from London.

For those living outside Boston, no doubt she would be prepared to make up a pack of traced canvas with the crewels to work it, complete with 'White Chapple Needles'. Other advertisements appearing in New England newspapers offer not only materials and patterns, but lessons in embroidery as well.

Plate 50. Framed panel. Collage, woven felted material, cut into shapes and arranged as a basket of fruit and flowers, with silk embroidery. Inscribed: *Worked by Elizabeth Catherine Sheath, wife of James Whiting Yorke of Walmsgate 1790*. Two other panels are known, with identical flowers and basket, but differently arranged. 48 × 43 cm. *Lady Victoria Wemyss*.

In Britain contemporary newspapers have not been combed with such devoted scholarship, but the existence of identical pieces of needlework in different parts of the kingdom suggests that prepared packs were known before the end of the eighteenth century. A delightful fabric collage, once thought to be felt, but now known to be of firmly woven woollen material, such as broadcloth, shows a basket of flowers containing auricula, passion flower, martagon lily and moss rose, was assembled and stitched in silk to a dark background in 1790 by Elizabeth Catherine Sheath, who married James Whiting Yorke of Walmsgate. (Plate 50.) Two other similar panels are known, with the same flowers, arranged differently in the same basket, each with attendant butterfly. One is at Mellerstain, Berwickshire, the other at Arniston, Midlothian. It would appear that these were all bought in ready-cut packs, prepared for assembly into a decorative panel for framing.

The Englishwoman's Domestic Magazine offered a useful service for those far from shops who wished to undertake the needlework designs issued as coloured plates. In June 1863, a Berlin wool pattern was published for a watch hook in the shape of a rose (to hold one's watch at night, pinned to the bed curtain). It was in raised wool work with an illustration and coloured chart on squared paper. The instructions tell how to work the stitches over a mesh, or gauge, to give the raised pile: '. . . the wool is not cut perfectly even and smooth, but in and out, and each petal is cut to give the rose as natural an appearance as possible . . .' 'Materials for working the hooks may be had of Mrs Wilcockson 44 Goodge Street, Tottenham Court Road, London W. for 2s 6d . . . Steel mesh 1s 3d.' The following month the *Sandringham Patchwork Pattern* was offered: green, white and orange hexagons with an interlace of red, blue and black patches. Again, Mrs Wilcockson was willing to supply 'Pieces of stiff paper or cardboard ready cut, and silk for completing the work' with prices on application.

While Mrs Wilcockson was supplying Victorian needlewomen at home and abroad with materials and threads for patchwork and Berlin wool work, at the same time William Morris was beginning to design large embroidered panels for churches and houses, together with furniture and stained glass. The firm of Morris Marshall Faulkener and Co. was founded in 1861. The embroideries, worked mainly on woollen or linen grounds, were a radical departure from the busy detail of a Berlin chart. The flowers and curving vegetation were the result of a conscious effort to recover what was thought to be the spontaneity of medieval needlework. These embroidered panels with their statuesque figures were designed as wall-hangings: an integral part of the complete furnishing of a room.

In 1885, William Morris's elder daughter May became head of the embroidery workshop, and continued after his death in 1896. As well as undertaking large commissions, special designs could be supplied, traced upon the fabric, together with silks for working. A child's bedspread survives, designed by May Morris and embroidered in 1889 by the American wife of a Scottish landowner, showing a house with garden containing delightful domestic birds and animals, with an American eagle soaring above surveying the scene. In the same showroom there were traced goods for sale, repeating designs by William Morris, and others by May: tablecloths,

Plate 51. Corner of square cover, worked in coloured silks on green silk damask. Bought ready traced with silks from Morris and Co. London, before 1914. Worked by Miss Alice Balfour of Balbirnie, Fife. Cover approx. 137 × 137 cm. *The late Miss Alice Balfour.*

cushion covers, blotters and teacosies, together with specially dyed silks to work them. 'They were so expensive' one old lady ruefully recalled 'that we took only a limited amount of money with us when we visited the shop'.[4] (Plate 51.)

Not every needlewoman could afford to buy Morris designs to work, but by the turn of the century designs, materials and threads were available in profusion. Hot iron transfers could be bought for white or coloured work, stamped designs on cloth were sold by many shops, including Liberty & Co. of Regent Street.

In spite of the teaching of Ann Macbeth and her students at the Glasgow School of Art, and other art schools where 'serious' embroidery was taught, many women still looked for a ready-drawn design to work, leaving them the choice of colour and stitches. Hand-painted canvas was imported from France and Austria, with wools for working. Sometimes, indeed, the central motif was already worked, leaving only the background to be filled in in monochrome. In 1926 the firm of William Briggs in Manchester, which had patented the hot iron transfer in 1874, began to market stencilled canvases together with Penelope wools in matching colours. The canvas was stencilled by hand. In 1948 the firm first marketed what were called *Penelope tapestry kits* with canvas wools and needle in the same pack. These designs are now screen printed on to the canvas in full colour.

The second world war was responsible for an unusual extension of the prepared pack of needlework. Although materials were rationed, and threads in short supply, unobtainable in the open market, the Red Cross with the help of the Embroiderers' Guild and other volunteers, made up packs that were sent to military hospitals and prisoner of war camps. These were by no means all ready traced: instructions were included showing how designs could be built up by counted thread methods. As a result of this modest introduction under the least favourable auspices, many men appreciated for the first time the absorbing fascination of stitchery and began a life-time involvement with this, one of the most civilised of skills.

References

1. The Letter Book of Samuel Sewell Vol. I 1686–1712 in *Collections of the Massachusetts Historical Society* 6th Series I (Boston 1886). I am indebted to Benno Forman of the Francis Henry du Pont Winterthur Museum for this reference.
2. Rowe A. P. Crewel embroidered Bed Hangings in Old and New England in *Boston Museum Bulletin* Vol. LXXI 1973 p. 112.
3. Quoted by G. Townsend *Bulletin of the Museum of Fine Arts Boston* 1942 pp. 111–115.
4. Miss Alice Balfour to the author in 1973.

TRANSFERRING THE DESIGN TO THE CLOTH

Plate 52. Engraving. French embroidery workroom, about 1770. The foreman, probably also the pattern drawer, is stretching a frame prior to tightening the lacing. A chasuble is marked out on the frame, which rests on a spar of wood (d) and a trestle. Two female embroiderers work at the other frame. One, left-handed, sits opposite from the right-handed worker. A pair of silk winders stand right (B) and on the wall hangs another frame (g) with two fronts of a gentleman's waistcoat marked out. From *L'Art du Brodeur* by M. St. Aubin.

1. Adjusting to size

When a significant and satisfying design has been chosen, there still remains the problem of transferring it to the cloth—linen, silk or canvas—for embroidering. In 1706 Rachel and Grisell Baillie with their governess, May Menzies, simply traced the lines of the flowers and creatures that they found in Thomas Johnson's book of engravings on to a rectangle of fine canvas, choosing them as they are drawn on the page. (Plates 10 and 11a.) As a result, the rose is taller than the swan, the kingfisher longer than the horse and the marigold stands on its head to fit into the existing

Plate 53. *A Phesant*. Coloured silks on canvas. Cross stitch. One of the panels at Oxburgh Hall that bears the initials M R (left, under the pheasant's throat) for Mary Queen of Scots. The design, which would not fit the cruciform shape, has been taken from Gesner's woodcut (Plate 54). *Victoria and Albert Museum on loan to Oxburgh Hall. Crown Copyright reserved.*

space. They were untroubled by problems of scale, but were content, like most needlewomen of their time, to get an accurate outline of the engraving on to the canvas.

Professional pattern drawers, with a large pile of engravings of different sizes to choose from, had to adopt other means to suit their patron's requirements. Canvas for the seat or back of a chair must be drawn to an exact size to fit comfortably within the frame, with sufficient canvas left all round for the upholsterer to turn in without cutting into the worked design. The vignette by Chauveau, for the French chair at Scone Palace (Plates 27 and 28) is only 7 × 8·5 cm (2¾ × 3½ in.) so that it was necessary to enlarge it, to fit the space. Often it was necessary to reduce the size of an engraving, or even to increase the height in relation to the width. Not everyone was willing to adopt the heroic solution to be found on the embroidery of *The Phesant* bearing the cypher of Mary Queen of Scots. There, in order to fit the cruciform shape of the panel, the long tail of the bird in Gesner's full-page woodcut has been cut in two with half the tail neatly laid above the bird. (Plates 53 and 54.)

The problem of transferring a design from a small sketch to a full-size cartoon has been encountered by artists from time immemorial. It is generally solved by drawing a grid of evenly spaced vertical and horizontal lines across the sketch and then drawing the same number of lines on to paper of the required size, and copying the outlines in each rectangle. This method has been adopted for large paintings, frescoes and tapestry cartoons. Leonardo da Vinci advised using this same method in order to get the proportions correct when drawing from life:

> If you wish thoroughly to accustom yourself to correct and good positions for your figures, fasten a frame or loom divided into squares by threads betwen your eyes and the nude

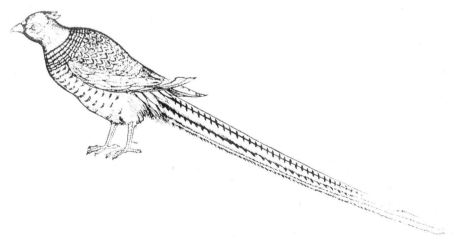

Plate 54. Woodcut. The Pheasant, from *Icones animalium* by Conrad Gesner, published in Zurich, 1560 edition. *The University of Edinburgh.*

figure which you are representing and then make the same squares upon the paper where you wish to draw the said nude but very faintly . . . The squares you draw may be as much smaller than those of the network in proportion as you wish your figure to be less than life size . . .[1]

Indeed, it has been suggested that the decorative chequered background of the figures on medieval manuscripts conceal the grid drawn by the illuminator who copied the scene from a drawing.

Today this method is still valid. It is helpful to cut a paper pattern to the exact size of the chair seat, bag, cushion or panel to be embroidered, on which the same number of squares or rectangles as the original can be drawn in pencil, *but very faintly*, in Leonardo's words. The lines within each square are then copied. This gives an idea of the full-size design (the *cartoon*) as it will appear on the cloth. It may need to be modified before the lines are inked in with a felt tip pen or transfer ink or pencil. It should be borne in mind that this cartoon is the *exact size* and extra material must be allowed for turnings and finishings, especially if the work is to be done in a frame or intended for upholstery, where a minimum of two inches at least must be left all round.

The size of canvas designs may be varied by using finer of coarser canvas, but it is essential to try out stitches and a motif on a sample before embarking on a large piece. A design that looks well on a fine count can look exceedingly clumsy on a large mesh, and may require considerable simplification to be acceptable.

Modern photography offers the simplest and quickest way to enlarge or reduce a design, and a commercial photographer, especially one dealing with advertisements, may be able to undertake this at a reasonable cost.

2. Drawn directly on to canvas or cloth

On old needlework, the inked outlines may still occasionally be glimpsed where the stitching has worn away, or the yarn has perished. They reveal a touching link with the embroiderer, showing the lines the needle followed so long ago. Many of the panels now at Oxburgh Hall, Norfolk, bearing the cypher of Mary Queen of Scots, show the inked lines where the black silk has perished, lines made by her embroiderer, who 'drew forth her designs' four hundred years ago. (Plate 4.)

We now know the source of these designs: which books were consulted, and which plates chosen. Moreover we know the source of many of the designs chosen for needlework pictures in the following centuries, as well as for embroidery to decorate the home: bed valances, hangings, chairs and screens. Once adapted to the correct size, the design had to be drawn out on to the fabric. (Plate 55.) This could be achieved in various ways, the simplest of which was to draw it directly on to the cloth. Only a skilled draughtsman would undertake this without a preliminary sketch, and fragile, pale or costly materials offered a hazard, so that other methods, pricking and pouncing, for instance, would be chosen. But transparent materials such as canvas, gauze, net or muslin, could be laid over the pattern and the outlines followed.

Plate 55. Canvas prepared for embroidery. The design has been drawn out on the fabric in ink. Some of the lines have been worked in black silk cross stitch in preparation for filling in with coloured tent stitch. *Mr Peter Maxwell Stuart of Traquair.*

Method

The full-size design to be copied (the *cartoon*) needs firm black outlines that can be seen through the top fabric.

1. Mark the centre lines of the cartoon horizontally and vertically.
2. Tack (baste) the centre lines of the material with running stitch, and position them over the cartoon, holding them both firmly by means of drawing pins or weights.
3. Follow the outlines using an indelible felt- or nylon-tipped pen, not an ordinary writing biro, which would 'bleed' if the work is damped while being blocked. For delicate fabrics a finely sharpened water colour pencil could be used. Anything *aquarelle* that smudges like ordinary lead pencil should be avoided.

Carbon paper

For the same reason, the needlewoman is usually warned against using carbon paper for transferring designs. Regular carbon paper is apt to smudge and mark the cloth in unwanted places. However, provided the correct carbon paper is used, successful results can be obtained. Coloured carbon paper (called *Tracing Paper*) is marketed for the use of dressmakers, and waxed paper in various colours is obtainable from artists' or architects' suppliers. I am indebted to Mildred J. Davis for permission to quote her method of tracing designs, using a very fine grade of carbon paper for electric typewriters:

Plate 56. Engraving. Lady making *parchment lace*. The outline threads are stitched to a strip of parchment, and a variety of fillings worked in the spaces. She wears an apron decorated with a rich border of such lace. Engraved and published by J. C. le Pautre (1617–82) Paris.

1. Draw or trace carefully the design as it is to be for the embroidery, using a good-quality tracing paper. Greaseproof paper is too thin.
2. Prepare material (i.e. linen or other similar material. This method is not used for canvas.)
3. The material should be smooth, no wrinkles. Place carbon with shiny side on to material . . . pin carefully around edges (margin where pin pricks will not show when embroidery is finished).
4. Place tracing paper with design on top of carbon and secure so that it will not slip.
5. Use a hard pencil, and by testing first, find out how hard to bear down to trace around the design. It is only necessary for a faint line to show.
6. For those who find difficulty in seeing the faint line, or who fear it may rub off in working, the line may be reinforced by a laundry marking pen (indelible). Ensure that this is quite dry before the embroidery is started, and as always, test first on scraps of the material.

3. Tacking to the pattern

For delicate transparent material it is often preferable to tack the design, drawn out on stiff paper or card, to the underside of the fabric, and use this as a support or guide while working the stitches. This is an ancient technique and was adopted for the making of point lace, made with a needle (as opposed to bobbin lace, made on a pillow). The lines of the pattern were drawn in ink on to vellum or parchment, and the outline threads of the lace tacked over the lines. The fillings of different looped stitches were then worked in the spaces, the edge generally buttonholed for extra strength and the scalloped border embellished with picots and other ornamental stitches. When complete, the tacking stitches were snipped at the underside of the vellum releasing the worked lace. Needlepoint lace was often called *parchment lace* in the past because of this method of working, as opposed to *bone* (bobbin) or pillow lace. (Plate 56.)

This was the method used by Mary Quelch who in 1609 began (but did not complete) a sampler of lace fillings, tacking thread to make rectangles for each different filling on to a strip of vellum, now stiff and curled with age.[2]

The same method was used by Henrietta Cumming (see p. 86) for the lappet and cap that she thought 'vastly pretty'. The stiff paper on which it has been drawn has been carefully tacked all round. Many of the patterns for muslin ruffles and fichus made under her direction are so tacked and appear to have been used several times. A partly-worked flounce of Dresden work (drawn muslin) tacked to a waxed paper (*toile ciré*) pattern is preserved in the Musées Royaux d'Art et d'Histoire at Brussels (no. 2562). A sleeve ruffle of the same period, the drawn muslin fillings showing an engaging variety, was probably also made in this way, the paper acting as support for the sheer muslin. (Plate 57.)

Thérèse de Dillmont, in the first edition of the *Encyclopaedia of Needlework*, still in print after a hundred years, suggests using stiff black paper with the design drawn

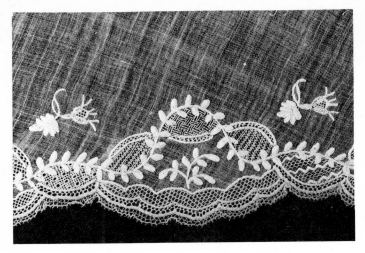

Plate 57. Sleeve ruffle (detail) late 18th century. White cotton on sheer muslin. Drawn muslin (*Dresden work*) outlined with chain stitch. The edging is unheaded bobbin lace. The muslin would have been attached to stiff paper on which the design was drawn for working.

in white as a basis for Venetian point lace.

Blue glazed architect's linen is the modern substitute for vellum, and has the advantage of being transparent, so that the drawn pattern can be traced on to it, but needlewomen far from the shops have, like Henrietta Cumming, made do with paper, sometimes backed with brown paper or calico to prevent it from tearing.

4. Pricking and pouncing

This is the most reliable and possibly the most ancient way of transferring a design on to cloth. The design must first be traced on to paper. Modern tracing paper, or greaseproof paper as a substitute, is sufficiently transparent to allow this to be done with ease, but in the past, when parchment or thicker paper had to be used, it was necessary to trace the design held against the light from a window, or, somewhat perilously, over a candle or lamp. (Plate 58.) The book used by the governess of Rachel and Grisell Baillie (see p. 33) shows that some of the flowers were traced with the book held against the glass of a window in this way.

Once the tracing was made, all the lines were pricked with a needle, making a row of fine holes. This pricked design was fastened over the stretched cloth and 'pounced'—that is, a pad of felt or flannel dipped in a powder was rubbed over the holes. On a dark material, powdered chalk, pumice or cuttle fish was used; on light fabric, charcoal. When the fabric was lifted, rows of fine dots of powder lay revealed.

Plate 58. Woodcut. Pricking and Pouncing.
Top left: tracing the design over a candle.
Top right: against the light of a window.
Bottom right: pricking the design. Bottom
left: pouncing the pricked design. On the
wall hang various other designs. Allesandro
Paganino *Il Burato* 1527.

These had to be 'fixed' with ink or paint. St Aubin, describing French workroom
practice of the 1770s, suggested using a fine pen made from the quill of a crow. Once
the lines were fixed, the surplus powder could be blown away.

Pricking and pouncing today
You will need
Chosen design of the correct size.
Tracing paper, larger than the fabric to be covered.
Sharpened pencil or fine ball point pen for tracing on to the paper.
A fine needle with the eye inserted into a cork (for ease of holding).
A strip of felt about 6 × 20 cm rolled like a bandage and tied firmly round the middle
to act as a pounce, or a pad of cotton wool.
Light or dark powder as required. (Dark: powdered charcoal or washing blue.
Light: powdered chalk or talcum powder).
A fine paint brush (size 000) and watercolour paint.
or a fine indelible felt- or nylon-tip pen.

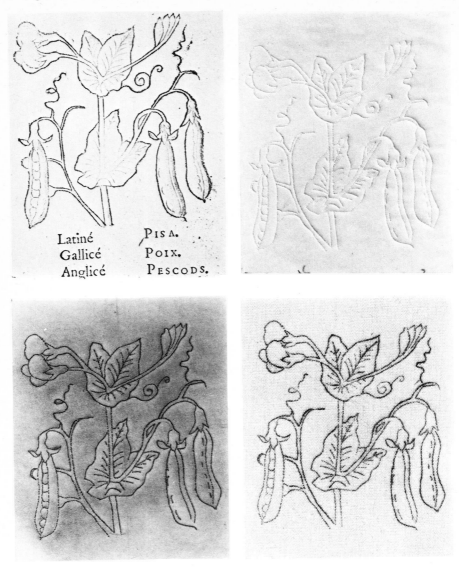

Plate 59. Pricking and pouncing. Top left: *Peascods*, a woodcut from *La Clef des Champs* by Jacques le Moyne 1586. Top right: Design pricked through tracing paper and laid over white cloth. Bottom left: The pricked paper has been rubbed with a pounce dipped in blue powder. Bottom right: the pricked design fixed with water colour.
Margery Hyde.

Method

1. Place the cartoon on a board or flat surface and rule through the centre horizontally and vertically. Mark these on the tracing paper and place over the design. Trace the design carefully making sure that all lines have been followed.
2. Turn the paper over (if the design is not symmetrical) and place the tracing paper with the design on it on to a padded board. Prick a row of close fine holes along each line with the needle. Extra copies can be made from the same pricking if several sheets of paper are placed underneath.
3. Stretch the fabric to be embroidered smoothly on a table, board or frame, marking the vertical and horizontal centre by means of tacking along the warp and weft thread. Turn the pricked design over. The holes will be seen slightly raised, like a nutmeg grater. Fix the paper down firmly with weights or drawing pins over the fabric, aligning the centre margins. *Allow sufficient material all round for turnings before pouncing.*
4. Rub the end of the roll of felt or a pad of cotton wool into the powder and rub gently along the lines, making sure that all are covered — use plenty of powder. Lift a corner to ensure that the lines are clearly marked. Remove the paper carefully, and trace over the powder dots with a fine brush and water colour or with the indelible ball point pen. *Not a biro.* Blow away surplus powder. (Plate 59.)

The method has changed very little since medieval times, except that a crow's quill is no longer easily obtainable. A ball point pen has superseded it, and the fine sable paint brush size ooo formerly used. Modern workrooms use an electric pricker that is operated rather like a dental drill. After pouncing, the powder, a commercial product, is fixed by using an aerosol spray of spirit, so that no further outlining is necessary.[3]

5. Counting squares

This is another ancient and trustworthy method, used on evenly woven material like canvas or linen. Some of the earliest pattern books printed designs on squares that could be counted and worked in cross stitch, Holbein stitch (double-running), cut work on linen, darned net (Lacis) or darned gauze (Burato). Many of these printed designs are very beautiful and can still be used today. (Plate 60.)

On the continent of Europe, especially in Germany, embroidery designs on squares continued to be printed in the eighteenth century (mostly small motives, like those found on samplers[4]) but in Britain they do not appear to have been used until the method received a new impetus in the nineteenth century with the arrival of Berlin patterns. They were, according to the Countess of Wilton in *The Art of Needlework* (1840), first published about 1804 by a print seller in Berlin called Philipson, who printed the designs on checked paper, the colours tinted by hand.

In 1810, Madame Wittich, who, being a very accomplished embroideress, perceived the great extension of which this branch of trade was capable, induced her husband, a book

Ce Pelican contient en longueur 70. mailles,
& en hauteur 65.

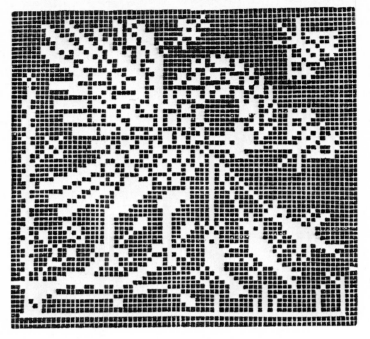

Plate 60. Design on squares, for darned net, plate from
Singuliers et Nouveaux Pourtraicts by Frederico Vinciolo, Paris
1606.

and print seller in Berlin, to engage in it with spirit. From that period the trade has gone on
rapidly increasing . . . By leading houses up to the commencement of the year 1840 there
have been no less than fourteen thousand copper plate designs published.

The wools imported to work these designs, a soft Saxony wool from the Merino
breed of sheep, dyed in Berlin and manufactured in Gotha, contributed in no small
way to the craze for Berlin wool work. Designs were included in ladies' magazines
in England, France and the United States by the 1860s. *The Englishwoman's
Domestic Magazine*, published by Sam Beeton, husband of Isabella Beeton, offered a
postal service whereby those living in the country could obtain materials for making
up the designs published. (Plate 61.)

The printing was fine, on small squares that the modern eye finds difficult to
count, but with perseverance, it was possible to obtain a far greater degree of realism
and fidelity to the chosen design than had been possible before. The soft wools with
their wider range of colours, not at first dyed with aniline compounds, added to the

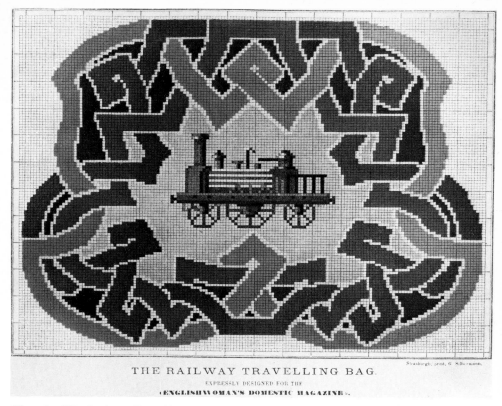

THE RAILWAY TRAVELLING BAG.

EXPRESSLY DESIGNED FOR THE

«ENGLISHWOMAN'S DOMESTIC MAGAZINE».

Plate 61. *The Railway Travelling Bag.* Design on squared paper in full colour published in the *Englishwoman's Domestic Magazine* June 1864. The engine to be worked in beads on a wool (cross stitch) background.

pleasure of embroidering favourite flowers: the rose, convolvulus and passion flower. What many condemn today are not the crude dyes of Berlin wool but the Victorian choice of colour. The belief still lingers that the vegetable dyes of earlier centuries were soft and subtle, although the colours we see today are altered and faded. The original reds, yellows and blues of the seventeenth century when seen unfaded are extremely vivid and would now be regarded as strident.

Realism was the aim of the Victorian embroideress, and the Berlin work designs were despised by succeeding generations whose taste was for more 'artistic' or impressionistic drawing. However, the use of squares for counting designs has continued to the present day, and pattern books using this convenient method are published in most western countries. Instead of colouring the squares, symbols showing the various shades are now used, with a key giving numbers or colours to follow.

For canvas work, a design charted on squares is considered superior to one drawn out on the canvas in ink, since each stitch is accommodated to the thread of the foundation.

To square out a design for canvas work
You will need:
Transparent graph paper (from an architect's supply firm)
Design of the correct size (for enlarging or reducing see p. 98)
Pencil, eraser, fine ball point pen.

Method
If the design is to be worked on a canvas of ten threads to the inch, transparent graph paper of that count should be used. This will give a worked design of the same size. Place the transparent squared paper over the design, and trace over the lines, but adjusting the curves to the grid so that each stitch can be counted. This results in a zig-zag instead of a curved line, but when worked, the design is accepted by the eye, and is much easier to follow than trying to work cross stitch along a drawn line which crosses theads at unequal intervals. Needlewomen of the past overcame this difficulty by working the inked lines in black silk cross stitch before filling in the colours. (See Plate 55.) The canvas was usually of a much finer count that that used commonly today.

When paper of the right count is unobtainable, a detail must be tried out on the linen or canvas before commencing the work. In all counted thread work, it is necessary to mark the vertical and horizontal centre lines by a tacking thread before beginning.

6. Printing with wood blocks

Carved wooden blocks, used for centuries in the orient and Europe for the printing of paper and cloth, do not appear to have been utilised for the printing of embroidery designs until the nineteenth century. It is true that one remaining worked design, in the Victoria and Albert Museum, is a replica of a piece of printed linen of the seventeenth century.[5] Marcus B. Huish in *Samplers and Tapestry Embroideries* illustrates (fig. 39, p. 131) an unworked satin picture of the same century, with an oval medallion which he describes as having deep incised lines coloured black. He suggests this might have been made with a stylus, but it could equally have been impressed by a block, especially since identical oval medallions are to be found on other pictures of the period.

Although most of the wooden blocks used for printing embroidery designs have gone up in smoke as firewood long ago, many museums in Europe and America still preserve examples. Without other evidence, it is not always clear whether these were used for printed fabric or for embroidery designs. In Scotland, wood blocks were employed for printing designs on cotton muslin to be embroidered in tambour

Plate 62a. Corner of the skirt of an infant's dress, bought 1859. White cotton on white muslin. Satin and lace stitches. An example of *Ayrshire embroidery* (sewed muslin). The repeat motives and the border design were stamped on the muslin by means of wooden blocks, and given to women to embroider in their own homes, before being returned to Glasgow for making up.

Plate 62b. Wooden blocks with copper strips inserted, used for stamping embroidery designs on to muslin. The design on the left hand block is a continuous line, suitable for tambour stitch. The spaces in the leaf border, right, would be completed with lace stitch fillings for Ayrshire embroidery. Scottish, about 1840. Left: 14·5 × 15 cm. Right: 4 × 9 cm.

stitch, continuous chain stitch, worked with a hook. A high standard of workmanship was demanded, and the patterns were drawn out by professional designers, trained in Edinburgh or Glasgow at the Drawing Academies set up by the Board of Trustees to improve the standards of industrial design.

A contemporary description runs:

> The blocks or prints are made of wood, generally sycamore, well seasoned and dried to prevent it from warping. The surface of the wood is planed smooth and very level and the pattern which is previously sketched on paper is traced on . . . The lines thus traced on the wood are left for making the impression, the intermediate spaces being scooped out with gouges or chisels . . . the colour generally employed for printing grey [unbleached] muslins is indigo, or Prussian blue. Goods which have been bleached and only require washing after they are tamboured, may be printed with rose-pink dissolved in water . . . Pipe-clay and water will be found of advantage for printing grounds of dark colours.[6]

Strips of lead or tin were often sunk into the blocks to produce a firmer outline. These wood blocks were a great convenience in printing the yards of scalloped edging and any repeat designs on the fine white needlework now known as Ayrshire embroidery, given to outworkers to embroider in their homes, a craft that flourished between 1830 and the end of the 1860s. (Plates 62a and 62b.)

Wooden blocks are said to have been used to print designs to be worked in feather or chain stitch on farm workers' smocks (round frocks) made for sale in Newark-on-Trent, Nottinghamshire, in the nineteenth century. Occasionally they were used to mark lines for quilting on bedcovers and petticoats. At Sturbridge Old Village, Massachusetts, blocks of various patterns survive, some with metal strips inserted, together with the quilting which they fit exactly. One 'block', however, is not wooden, but an ingeniously made substitute. On thin stiff cardboard, the parallel lines of the 'cable' or 'twist' pattern have been meticulously drawn on to two interlocking shapes, and cord has been stitched firmly along each line. The impression of the cords, now white with the remains of pipe-clay or chalk, was retained by the material to be quilted. A brown silk quilted petticoat bears this cable border, though no mark survives either on the surface or back to show how this home-made printing device was used.

About five hundred embroidery blocks are preserved in the Wenham Historical Association and Museum, Massachusetts, made, not of sycamore, but of rock maple with pine laminates, many with strips of copper, brass or pewter inserted. They belonged to an enterprising young woman, Philena Clarinda Moxley, who bought some secondhand in 1867 from William Leland, the owner of an embroidery printing shop where she worked, at Lowell, Massachusetts. Philena had been taught the use of these blocks by Leland's partner William Chambers, who had brought some from Britain when he emigrated around 1840. Philena Moxley set up in business as an embroidery stamper on her own account in 1868, and in 1871 took out a mortgage and built a printing shop, a store selling fancy goods, and a house. Her business flourished: she stamped hessian (burlap) for hooked rugs, as well as material for underwear and dress, for which she sold paper patterns. She remained in business till 1889, after she had married a widower with two sons, and had two daughters of her own. She died in 1937 at the age of ninety-four.[7] The blocks show flower sprays, initials, designs for braiding and many fine scalloped edgings for baby clothes and underwear. The larger blocks for rugs were used to fire her furnace during a coal strike.

In America, Godey's *Lady's Book* published an advertisement in 1859 offering blocks for sale 'Adapted to silk as well as the French embroidery, and will stamp upon any material with white or blue ink with the greatest accuracy'. Wooden stamps, repetitive, laborious and requiring a degree of skill in use, were superseded by the invention of the iron-on transfer for the domestic needlewoman. Commercial firms now use more up-to-date methods of printing embroidery designs on to cloth.

7. Iron-on transfers

A cleaner, simpler method of printing embroidery designs on to cloth, one that could be undertaken by any domestic needlewoman, began with the introduction of iron-on transfers. The process, invented by three employees of William Briggs of Manchester in 1875, consisted of printing the pattern on to thin paper with a bituminous ink, the lines of which adhered to the cloth when the wrong side of the paper was pressed with a hot iron. For the yards of scalloped edgings worked on baby linen and underwear, and for household linens, this was a great advance. Initials and sprays, bought for a few pence, could be cut and arranged to the taste of the needlewoman. The choice was wide; needlework shops kept books or boxes filled with transfers. In London, Liberty and Co. offered *Original Designs for Home Needlework* in the style of Art Noveau, and the Embroiderers' Guild sold transfers of approved design, whilst women's magazines often included a free transfer in an issue together with instructions for working. Although the fashion for hand-embroidered underwear and household linens has somewhat abated, it is still possible to buy transfers, which are often included in needlework publications.

There are now both single-impression and multi-print transfers available. The latter are useful for sets of table linen, or repeat motives. The multi-print can give up to eight impressions on fine fabric, fewer on thicker fabric which absorbs more of the ink. In using transfers, it is always necessary to test the heat of the iron by trying out the lettering and numbers (printed on the transfer) on a scrap of similar fabric first. This is especially important if using a synthetic material, since many of them shrivel or melt if too hot an iron is applied, whereas too cool an iron will fail to transfer the ink to the material. A steam iron is not recommended. Home-made transfer ink can be made as follows:

You will need:
For light materials
1 level teaspoon of Reckitt's blue, powdered
3 level teaspoons of castor sugar
White tissue paper

For dark materials
1 level teaspoon of precipitated chalk
3 level teaspoons of castor sugar
Blue or other coloured tissue paper
These mixtures should be kept in small screw-topped jars till required for use.

To use
1. Mix 4 parts of either mixture with one part of boiling water before use. Mix freshly each time. A saltspoon is a large enough measure to mix the small quantity required. The design should be lightly drawn or traced on to the chosen tissue paper.
2. With a fine nib, dipped into the well-stirred mixture, go over the lines carefully, remembering that any errors will iron off on to the cloth. Make a few crosses at the edge for trial transfers, and leave to dry.
3. First test the crosses and the heat of the iron on a scrap of the material.
4. Iron the cloth first to press out all wrinkles, then apply the transfer carefully, pinning in place, and press, do not rub, with the iron, so that the design is evenly transferred. The paper can be re-inked for use again, but should not be stored ready inked, as humidity will cause the design to become sticky.

Transfer ink can be bought, and a transfer pencil is now on the market[8] which is cleaner to use; moreover the tracing and inking require only one operation. It is essential to keep the point well sharpened, otherwise the lines become too thick. The pencil is apt to flake. Any loose fragments should be carefully shaken off before using the transfer, otherwise they will appear on the cloth.

8. Tacking through tissue paper

Some materials, particularly woollens or fabrics with a pile, will not accept transfer or carbon paper readily, and cannot be pricked and pounced. For these the design is stitched through paper.

Method
1. Trace the design on to good quality tissue paper or thin tracing paper.
2. Attach to the stretched cloth, centre to centre as before.
3. Stitch along the traced lines through the paper and cloth, using short tacking (basting) stitches with a contrasting thread. It is helpful if every third stitch is a back stitch. Fasten off firmly.
4. When all the lines have been covered by the stitches, slit the paper along the stitch lines with the point of the needle and gently tear away, a little at a time, leaving the tacking threads as outline. Great care is needed to ensure that the threads are not displaced when the tissue is removed. The embroidery may cover them, or they

can be withdrawn when the work is finished by snipping through a short portion at a time. This method has much to commend it, since no mark is made upon the material.

9. Templates and stencils

Templates, or templets, are used by builders, carpenters and engineers as well as by needlewomen. They are gauges or moulds used to produce exact dimensions in repeats of a given design. They are widely employed in patchwork and quilting, or in marking curves or scallops along a border.

The simplest are for circles. Elegant designs have been produced in the past, using only coins, wine-glasses or saucers. Even without geometry, a square of folded paper will result in angled shapes for patchwork or a design in counted thread; a narrow strip of card will keep intersecting lines straight and even. But for more ambitious patchwork the design should be charted on squared or isometric[9] graph paper. The shapes can be cut and used as templates. More permanent templates can be cut out from card, tin or plastic, either to order, or from specialist needlework shops.

Some needlewomen cut out the shapes of their chosen design in stiff paper, or a thin-gauge acrylic, drawing around these templates, instead of pricking and pouncing, or transferring by some other method.

Stencils may also be used to mark designs on to cloth. At the Glasgow School of Art, both Mrs Newbery and Ann Macbeth used this method for repeating designs. Stiff oiled paper or thin card (often used for making lampshades) was marked with the chosen design and laid upon glass so that the spaces could be cut away with a sharp knife. The resulting stencil was laid on the cloth and a piece of velvet, damped in watercolour, was dabbed over the stencil to mark the spaces. When dry, these were covered with stitchery.

10. Samplers

John Palsgrave's definition of a sampler in his English–French dictionary of 1530, *Exampler for a woman to work by; exemple* has been often quoted. It suggests a strip of linen with fragments of needlework patterns, recorded like cookery receipts copied down or borrowed from friends and stored for future use. The early 'spot' samplers of the seventeenth century certainly offer a selection of worked motives; like the Berlin work samplers of the nineteenth century they may be regarded as a selection of patterns made by an adult. They are trial pieces suggesting colours and threads of the type that most needlewomen experiment with before embarking on a major piece of embroidery. Very occasionally, a bag or a cap (Plate 63a and b) may be found, worked in a design that recalls these 'spot' motives, though most must have disintegrated in use.

Plate 63a. Man's cap. Gold and silver metal threads and spangles. Rococo stitch. 17th century. *Grimsthorpe and Drummond Castle Trust.*

To most people, a sampler now suggests a schoolgirl's piece, complete with alphabet, name and date, that changed remarkably little through the years, just as Helen Webster's, made as late as 1852 in Largo, Fife, shows. (Plate 64.) The sampler had become, indeed, the traditional means of teaching a child the alphabet and 'marking stitch' for linen. The colours must have made it a welcome change from the tedium of plain hemming. These charming and often touching panels, framed and glazed, have been widely collected for the past eighty years, but they cannot be regarded as pattern sources: they are, with few exceptions, patterns transferred by counting squares (see p. 107). Most of them are profoundly conservative, handed down as they were from one generation to another.

Trade samplers, that is, examples of embroidery that could be worked to order, are less common, since they were usually discarded when fashion changed, or a firm went out of business. Since most professional embroiderers had a draughtsman or woman skilled at drawing out designs, they are generally of a very high standard. Underwear, handkerchiefs and household linen all bore the owner's initials. In

Plate 63b. A detail shows the S motives often found on 'spot' samplers of the 17th century, worked in rococo stitch.

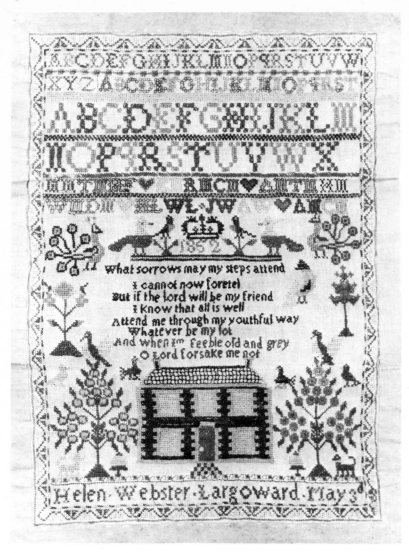

Plate 64. Sampler by Helen Webster, Largoward, Fife 1852. Coloured wools on linen canvas. Cross stitch. Although made in the middle of the nineteenth century, this neatly-worked sampler repeats traditional Scottish motives: the border, birds in a tree and the peacock with seven tail feathers have been handed down for over a century without alteration. *Mrs Webster.*

France, the *Lingère* provided (and still provides) these to order. Sketches from an Edinburgh firm active around 1839 to 1939, and worked examples from Belfast, show how charming these were. (Plate 65.)

Plate 65. Trade sampler. Initials and other motives worked on fine linen, from the firm of Mrs and Miss Bowie, muslin printers and embroiderers, Princes Street, Edinburgh from 1839 to 1939. *The National Museum of Scottish Antiquities.*

11. Embroidery frames

The material must be held taut while being decorated with stitches, to prevent pulling or puckering. The most elementary way to achieve this is to stretch the fabric over the fingers of one hand, holding it firmly by the thumb, while wielding the needle in the other hand. In the past, a firmly padded small cushion was used, to which one end of the material could be pinned. Sometimes a table clamp may be found, with a small pincushion on top. Using this, it is possible to stitch hems very evenly and rapidly.

It is impossible, however, to work some types of embroidery without holding the fabric taut in a frame. There are now two shapes available: the tambour or hoop

Plate 66. Engraving *La Pres Disner*. The seated lady works at a
cylindrical frame, the lady standing is making a piece of lace on
parchment. Engraved and published by N. Arnoult, Paris. Late 18th
century. *The Pierpont Morgan Library, New York.*

frame, and the rectangular frame, though in the past, cylindrical frames were used. (Plate 66.)

The tambour frame
The tambour frame was introduced into Europe around 1760, along with the tambour needle.[10] The latter, like a fine crochet hook, had been used in India to execute fine even chain stitch, where the thread, held beneath the material, was hooked up in a continuous line. This was quicker and easier to work than chain stitch made with needle and thread, and rapidly became the vogue in Europe and America. In 1763 Madame de Pompadour had her portrait painted at this fashionable pursuit by François Drouais, but for her tambour work she chose the traditional rectangular frame rather than the round 'drum' frame. When Horace Walpole commissioned Sir Joshua Reynolds in 1780 to paint his grand nieces, the Ladies Waldegrave, he desired a portrait of the Three Graces, posed around a column surmounted by a bust of their mother, his niece. Instead, they chose to be painted seated at a table with Lady Horatia at her tambour frame, her two sisters winding the silk for working. (Plate 67.) Schools for young ladies taught tambour work as an elegant accomplishment. In Scotland at the end of the eighteenth century, workshops were set up for the tambouring of white cotton muslin, worked by young girls. They did not, however, use the round frame of the amateur. A heavy wooden frame survives in the David Livingstone Museum, Blantyre, capable of taking a whole web of muslin, at which four girls could sit two on either side, to cover the surface rapidly with their tambour hooks.

The round frame should only be used for small pieces of embroidery, mainly white work, or silk, though it ought to be used with great caution for the latter, which is apt to crease, even if the inner ring be padded. It should never be used for any embroidery worked by counting threads, as it is necessary in that case to have the warp and weft threads held at right angles, and this requires a rectangular frame.

The rectangular frame
The rectangular frame goes back to antiquity, (Plate 68), and was the *tent* or *tenter* on which cloth was stretched, either for weaving, bleaching or embroidering. Basically it consists of two beams or cross bars, with side spars that hold the beams rigid and to which the selvedges can be lashed. (Plate 69.) In 1587, among the items left behind in Edinburgh Castle by Mary Queen of Scots during her captivity in England were 'Certane werklumes for ane brodinstare' (frames for an embroiderer), while in 1601, the Countess of Shrewsbury, Bess of Hardwick, stored 'nyne payre of beams for imbroderers' in a small room at Hardwick Hall.

Rectangular frames vary in size, from those large enough to take a bedcover for quilting, to one small enough to stretch a netted square of a few inches for darning a pattern through its meshes. They may be simple slate-frames or well-turned and polished floor-frames with a stand sufficiently elegant to grace a drawing room.

The amateur needlewoman is often reluctant to use a frame, partly because it

Plate 67. Painting *The Ladies Waldegrave* by Sir Joshua Reynolds. Lady Horatia (right) holds a round frame with the tambour hook in her right hand, the ball of thread in her left hand underneath. Her sisters wind the silks. Painted 1780–81. *The National Gallery of Scotland.*

makes the work less portable, but chiefly because the correct 'dressing' of a frame is regarded as difficult and abstruse, suitable only for the expert. Once the principles are understood, the use of a frame makes it infinitely easier to work evenly without distortion.

For a small piece of canvas work, such as a spectacle case, a slate frame of four pieces of wood with right angled corners may be used, the canvas held down by drawing pins (thumb tacks) pushed through the holes of the canvas (not the threads) to hold the warp and weft threads straight.

Plate 68. Wood cut. The Story of Arachne, from Ovid's *Metamorphoses* illustrated by Bernard Salomon. Arachne, famous for her spinning and weaving, challenged Minerva to compete with her. She wove a tapestry showing the loves of the gods. Punished by Minerva, she tried to hang herself, and was turned into a spider. Salomon's woodcut shows them embroidering, not weaving, and using rectangular needlework frames. In the background, Arachne, hanging herself, is being changed into a spider by Minerva. *The Warburg Institute, London.*

To dress a rectangular or slate frame

These frames consist of four pieces with four wooden pegs or split pins. The two rollers have a strip of webbing nailed down their length. The centre of each roller should be marked. The two stretchers are flat laths with a line of holes bored through them. The stretchers fit through the holes at the end of the rollers.

The grain of the fabric should run from roller to roller: the selvedge sides should face the stretchers.

1. Mark the half-way point between the two selvedge sides to ensure that the fabric is centred. Turn in a small hem at the top and bottom of the fabric starting from the centre mark of the webbing and fabric and sew together.

(a) 'Tapestry' hand frame with adjustable sides.

(b) Rotating or travel frame.

Plate 69. Rectangular needlework frames. (a) 'Tapestry' hand frame with adjustable sides. (b) Rotating or travel frame. (c) Rectangular floor frame. *Messrs. J. and P. Coats.*

2. When the work is oversewn to one roller, attach the other end to the second roller in the same manner.
3. Then sew a strip of tape to each of the two selvedge edges, using herringbone stitch. If the material is longer than the stretchers, the excess may be wound round one of the rollers, protected by a piece of muslin or linen during winding.
4. The stretchers are then inserted into the holes at the ends of the rollers, and pegged as far apart as they will stretch. The placing of the pegs on one side must match with those on the other side.
5. Attach a strong thread to the top of each lath and lace through the side tapes around the stretchers for the length of the fabric. The threads are then knotted round the bottom of the laths to be undone and retightened if necessary.

Some slate frames have legs attached to the stretchers which make them floor frames or table frames.

Certain frames have stretchers fitted with wooden screws, giving the advantage of tightening or slackening the fabric while work is in progress.

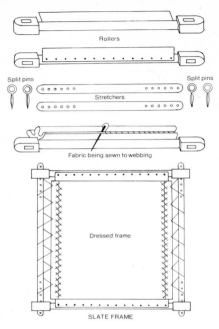

References

1. MacCurdy E. J. *The Notebooks of Leonardo da Vinci* Cape 1938 Vol. II p. 254.
2. In the collection of Dr Douglas Goodhart. See: Swain M. H. *Historical Needlework* 1970 pl. 54.
3. I am indebted to Messrs J. & P. Coats, Glasgow for this information.
4. e.g. Martin Engelbrecht (1684–1756) published in Augsburg small designs for embroiderers.
5. Wace A. J. B. Embroidery in the collection of Sir Frederick Richmond, Bart. in *Apollo* XVII 1933 Figs VIII and IX.
6. *Encyclopaedia Edinensis*, or the *Dictionary of the Arts, Sciences and Literature* Edinburgh 1827 Vol. II p. 458.
7. Dodge I. Philena Moxley's embroidery stamps in *Antiques* August 1972 pp. 251–252.
8. Transfer Ink. Made by Dryad Handicrafts, Leicester. Transfer Pencil by Lowe & Carr Ltd. Liberty Works, Eastern Boulevard, Leicester LE2 7BG.
9. A paper printed with equilateral triangles instead of squares, obtainable from architects' supply shops.
10. St Aubin, M. de *L'Art du Brodeur* Academie des Sciences, Paris 1770 p. 27.
11. I am indebted to Evelyn Wylie for her description and sketch of dressing a frame.

INDEX